# Strength Without Compromise:
## Womanly Influence and Political Identity in Turn-of-the-Twentieth Century Rural Upstate New York

### Teri P. Gay

To my friends Judy & Bill —

Enjoy!

Love,
Teri
11-14-12

Teri P. Gay

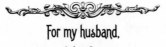

For my husband,
John Gay
My heart, my soul, and my love

# Strength Without Compromise:
## Womanly Influence and Political Identity in Turn-of-the-Twentieth Century Rural Upstate New York

### FIRST EDITION 2009

ISBN 978-0-9842215-0-9

Published by The American Classics and Design Co.
Malta, New York 12019
Teri P. Gay
2009

Produced by New York Press & Graphics, Inc.
Albany, New York 12205

Printed in Canada

# TABLE OF CONTENTS

# TABLE OF CONTENTS

# ILLUSTRATIONS

# ACKNOWLEDGEMENTS AND METHODOLOGY

I am very indebted to the many people who have helped me over the course of the almost thirty years in which this book was being researched and transforming into what you hold in your hands today. The focus of my inquiries took some circuitous routes over time and yet the goal remained unchanged: to tell the story of the women's suffrage movement in the smaller, rural, and lesser known communities of upstate New York where I was born and grew to adulthood.

The attachment to the women I have studied is equal to my attachment to this region that has always been my home, except for a decade (1980 – 1990) when I lived and worked in Connecticut. It is very true that the tug of home lives like a compass inside me; it always has. In my case, the years of my life, the important people in my life, and my life's work have all been products of my geography. This is, in part, why my book's focus – although thematically about women's rights in a rural setting -- is more the story of a certain women's group in a particular town, close to my hometown.

This is the story of the Easton Political Equality Club (PEC) in the little town of Easton, Washington County, New York and its two dynamic leaders, Lucy Allen and Chloe Sisson. This book will describe what happened with these particular women and their fellow PEC members, whose motivation and momentum were very much products of *their* environment and of their own attachment to their land, their farming community, and the relationships with their families and neighbors that formed the framework of their day-to-day lives. This model is my rubric; it is the foundation for this book and its symbolic purpose as the prism through which other smaller, not well known, and yet highly effective women's suffrage groups can be examined.

It is a model for my own life, too, which is very much the result of the powerful influences of my sense of place here in upstate New York. Intrinsic to my happiness and fulfillment, along with my ability to do good, productive work, is that *where* I live, and the people with whom I am surrounded, motivate and inspire me in everything I do, including in the writing of this book.

So many of the people who assisted my early efforts as a college girl on her winterterm project in 1980 – how this book was born – were the same people (older now, to be sure) who answered more questions or gathered more files for me in 2003 through 2009, as the final book was coming to fruition. My reliance on these trusted associates in turning out this book is the proof of what I wrote above: simply that there is comfort in the familiarity of people and place, and that this blend of connection of human beings to their environment and to their land brings great possibilities for human endeavor and for a lasting legacy. Hopefully this book demonstrates and lives up to that.

I have been blessed by such people in my own life here, and I thank them tremendously – not only for the tasks or tangible assistance they provided to me – but also for their friendship, camaraderie, and caring, and for indulging me in my excitement about my project. Sadly, some of the original contributors to my research have passed on, but their parts in this book are significant, if only for igniting in me the urge to dig and delve further and further into the story of the women's rights movement in the upstate New York area – and why it happened *this* way *here*.

From the early days of the genesis of this book, Joe Cutshall-King was a guiding force and also a mentor. It was he who, as the then-Executive Director of the Chapman Historical Museum in Glens Falls, Warren County, New York, monitored my college project on behalf of St. Lawrence University in Canton, New York. That internship resulted in a paper which became my first little book – *The Woman Suffrage Movement in the Glens Falls Area* – which is still part of the Chapman's collection today. Joe, originally from Fort

Edward in neighboring Washington County, was one of the main reasons I became an historian and a writer in the first place, for, by his own example, he caused in me the realization that my passion for regional history was to be my life's calling (albeit after some twists and turns in careers). He was proud of me when I needed encouragement, wrote about my research on local women in his newspaper column, and indulged my endless questions and inquiries on all matters of Warren, Washington, and Saratoga counties history over three decades. He is today the director of development at Adirondack Community College in Queensbury and still writes brilliantly about local history in his spare time. He was and is for me that important touchstone that hopefully each of us is privileged to have in life, whom we meet at a pivotal juncture, inspiring and guiding us like a North Star into our destined productive endeavors. I thank Joe Cutshall-King tremendously for the shove he gave me way back when to do what I do today.

I cannot believe I was lucky enough to have *a second* touchstone in my life– Dr. Marilyn Van Dyke, Executive Director of the Warren County Historical Society and Queensbury Town Historian. My good fortune in meeting Marilyn in 2002 has led to a friendship and professional association that is unique and special to me. It was Marilyn who encouraged me to finish my book about women's suffrage, and she published my article, "Suffrage and Feminist Reform In and Around Warren County" in the Warren County Historical Society's journal, *Pasttimes*, in the fall of 2004. She nurtured my continued research in the field of women's rights in our region, listened to me talk on and on and on about my theories and hypotheses about the interconnections of the women's suffrage movement with other 19th century reformist movements, like temperance and abolition, in our region. She challenged me and pushed me, and, by her example as a wife, mother, businesswoman, and academician who returned to college in her forties to earn her Ph.D, she showed me the way to achieve the blend of the mother-writer-historian life. She trained me as a public historian when, in 2004, I was appointed Historian for the Town of Malta, Saratoga

County, and we commiserated about our roles as dedicated advocates for history in two similar rural, yet evolving, towns, where politics seeped into our purist efforts. She was my angel when she agreed to read drafts of this book and to help me shape it into a worthy final product. Through it all, we shared so much of our lives together, professional and personal, serving as one another's balcony people, lifting each other up as women striving to fulfill our potentials. A century ago, Marilyn and I might have been the Lucy Allen and Chloe Sisson of Glens Falls, leading the charge for political equality for women in our hometown. I thank Marilyn for so much. She has given me the gift of her knowledge, experience, and tenacity, and I flatter myself on occasion by thinking that some of her remarkable talents and qualities might have rubbed off onto me.

From the days of my initial research in 1980, I wish to thank Paul McCarty, then and now the Historian for the Village of Fort Edward and the Executive Director of The Old Fort House Museum in historic Fort Edward, Washington County, New York. Also offering information and insight on the women's suffrage movement in Fort Edward and Hudson Falls were Esther Sherman, Erskine Rogers, and James Cronkhite. Edgar Snyder of Greenwich and Mrs. Gordon MacEachron of Argyle offered valuable information on suffrage activities in Washington County. Fast forward to 2008, and Mary Jane Ellis, research librarian of the John Burke Research Center, part of The Old Fort House, who set aside hours of her time to gather materials for me on Elizabeth Wakeman Mitchell and Laura Schafer Porter, was a godsend.

In 1980, I was privileged to correspond with Ernst McAneny of Bronx, New York, who shared remembrances about the suffrage work of his grandmother, Dr. Mary Putnam Jacobi, whom Warren County can claim as one of its own because of her summer residency at Bolton Landing on the prestigious "Millionaire's Row," as the mansions along Route 9N from Lake George to Bolton are called. Joan Robertson of Cleverdale on Lake George offered insights on her ancestors' participation in suffrage activities in Warren County and Glens Falls. Mrs. Carter (Hilda Tait) Hall, whose father was the founder of the Imperial Company (wallpaper and chemicals) in Glens Falls, who was in her eighties in 1980, wrote me a lively letter from her home in Stamford, Connecticut describing the suffrage activities she had been a part of in the 1910's in the city of Glens Falls. Also in 1980, Stephen Birdsall spent an afternoon with me in his lovely Queensbury home recounting the suffrage teas attended by and hosted by his suffragist grandmother, Mrs. Edgar Birdsall, in Glens Falls as the State Referendum on woman suffrage neared in 1917. Other Glens Falls residents who offered information and insight to me were: John Austin, Dora Bullock, Mrs. William Bowden, Robert Eddy, Donald Hallenbeck, Rachel Harrington, and Margaret Krarup. In 2004, I was pleased to interview Dan Robertson and his sister Alice Robertson Peabody about the suffrage activities of their grandmother, Mrs. Daniel Robertson, in Glens Falls.

I was aided generously by the assistance of: Tim Weidner, Executive Director of the Chapman Historical Museum in Glens Falls, and Jillian Mulder, the curator of the Chapman; Kristina Saddlemire, Saratoga County Historian; Jane Meader Nye, whose knowledge of Quaker history makes her a much sought after resource; Joy Houle, Executive Director of the Brookside Historical Museum in Ballston Spa, Saratoga County, and Kathleen Coleman, the curator of Brookside, and Joan Dunseath, a respected volunteer historian at Brookside.

In 2008, I was grateful for the assistance of Linda Palmieri and Linda Sanders, Historians for the Town and Village, respectively, of Stillwater in Saratoga County; and, Teri Blasko, History Librarian, and Victoria Garlanda, research assistant, both of the Saratoga Room in the Saratoga Springs Public Library. Also of great help were: Barbara Anderson, librarian, and Catherine Taylor, former librarian, at the Washington County Historical Association; Loretta Bates, Washington County Historian; and the staff of the Greenwich Library, Washington County.

I am also very grateful to Laura Lee Linder, Charlton Town Historian, in Saratoga County, for going the extra mile in gathering information about Brooklyn and Warren County suffragist, Mary Hillard Loines. Laura and her husband Clarence own a summer home in Bolton Landing that was once part of the Loines' summer estate on Lake George. Nancy Dalton Rogal, a descendent of the Loines family, who lives in what was once called the "Crow's Nest" on that property, was gracious enough to provide valuable photos, information, and insight on Mary Hillard Loines through Laura.

Linda Lumsden, Associate Professor at Western Kentucky University and author of a noted biography of famous suffragette Inez Milholland, and of *Rampant Women*, an excellent history of how suffragists employed the right of assembly in their quest for enfranchisement, was a great inspiration to me. I met her in the small, far north Adirondack town of Elizabethtown, in Essex County, New York in August 2004 when I heard her speak about her new book, *Inez: The Life and Times of Inez Milholland*. Inez was a charismatic young suffragist who had dazzled America with her speeches and writings about women's rights and with her grace and beauty as she rode atop a white horse as herald of the historic suffrage parade in Washington D.C. in 1915. Linda signed copies of both of her books for me on that August day and spoke with me about my own book project on women's suffrage. That brief encounter will always be a magical moment in my life, when the dream of a book of my own became blessed by a distinguished author with a passion for women's history that matched my own.

Three ladies of Easton deserve grandiose praise for their part in helping me bring the story of Lucy Allen, Chloe Sisson, and the Easton PEC to light. First, Earline Houser, Historian for the Town of Easton, responded to my written plea in 2004 for information about the women's suffrage movement in Easton with a plethora of newspaper articles she had dug up for me with detective work befitting the finest historian! It was she who first introduced me to Lucy and Chloe and their extraordinary political equality club. I will never be able to fully thank Earline for what her sharing all of this with me has meant, for her contribution to my research was the "lightbulb moment" in the synthesis of my thinking about the special brand of suffrage work carried on by rural women in this region at the turn of the 20th century.

Second, Helen Brownell, librarian of the Easton Library, and who, like her school classmate Earline Houser has been a lifelong resident of bucolic Easton, was my partner through months of research on site at the library. There, I read the minutes books of the Easton PEC's meetings and examined files, books, and materials about the history of the town, the Grange, and the Women's Christian Temperance Union, along with the letters, speeches, and writings of PEC leaders, Lucy Allen and Chloe Sisson. I am eternally grateful to Helen for taking huge amounts of time to gather files and information, answer all my questions, and indulge my quest. I also thank her for being as excited as I was all along the way that the incredible story of the Easton PEC would finally be told.

My third special lady of Easton is Library Trustee Mary Jane Connor, who had been in the class ahead of mine at St. Lawrence University and who I met up with again quite by chance at my favorite coffee shop in Greenwich back in 2004. Mary Jane and I quickly reconnected, and I discovered her interest in women's history when she spoke of a project she and Helen Brownell were spearheading – "Honor the Ladies," a tribute to none other than Lucy Allen and Chloe Sisson and the remarkable ladies of the Easton PEC! She and her committee organized a delightful evening of history, music, and exhibition in celebration of the PEC and its members and their influence on the cause of women's suffrage in Washington County in the late 19th century and early 20th century. Mary Jane invited me to attend this important event, held on October 2, 2004, and I became further captivated by these rural women who had done so much for the effort to gain female political equality.

A century after the founding of the Easton PEC, I see the extraordinary blend of feminine grace and brilliance of Lucy, Chloe, and their fellow members exemplified in the new generation of female town leaders: Earline, Helen, and Mary Jane. I am reminded, in the lives and works of all of these women that civic achievement of women, along with community and political influence, need not mean sacrificing what is womanly. For indeed, that is the crux of this book. Womanly influence and political identity of the female population are indeed both at the core of our strength as women and as citizens *and* they are the products of that strength.

Without compromising the very essence of their womanliness, femininity, and ladylike qualities, these ladies (then and now) of Easton showed enormous strength, influence, and achievement. As such, they serve as timeless models for the integration of gender-specific qualities in the quest for the creation of a better world.  In addition, they may just offer a new and exciting paradigm for feminism that does not seek to frame women's struggles for equality as a monolithic journey couched in the rhetoric of oppression and the language of gender-neutral verbiage, but rather the possibility for the supporting of women who show us how femininity, intellect, citizenship, and humanity can coalesce – without compromise – and produce highly functioning girls and women for a society which celebrates the needed contributions of both genders in order to meet the challenges of a complex future and to leave a legacy that is rich in promise for gender, racial, ethnic, and age tolerance and diversity.  I thank Earline, Helen, and Mary Jane for showing me the way to Lucy and Chloe and the rest of the remarkable women of the Easton Political Equality Club at the turn of the 20th century.

I thank also John Slocum and Norman Allen of Easton for giving permission for the use of photographs of Chloe Sisson and Lucy Allen.

I also thank Paul W. Sickles, creator and President of The American Classics Company, for his publishing and marketing genius and for hooking onto the concept of "strength without compromise" as the perfect title for this book.  His guidance, advice, and creative brilliance made this book a better product than it ever would have been without him.

I want to thank my three sons – Benson, Viggo, and Marshall Ulrich – who are the finest sons a mother could wish for and who inspire me everyday to lead my life with the knowledge that I am able to do my best work as a writer and historian only because of the fulfillment I get from being a mother and a wife. Talented writers themselves, they teach me something everyday. They know well that I am crazy about them, and their love is precious to me.

My greatest thanks goes to my husband, John Gay. It was he who encouraged me to focus my professional time solely on this project and made it possible for me to lead the self-absorbed life of a creative person through the duration. He made fires to keep me warm as I wrote, sat silently nearby to keep me company as my pen flew across the paper, listened to me expound and gush and wallow and worry, and gave me the rock-solid guidance and direction that has made him an extraordinary engineer and company president over many years. John is my partner in life and in all things, who has given me unwavering support in the creation of this book and in everything I do. My love, admiration, and respect for him are boundless, and I truly thank him for inspiring me, believing in me, and loving me so.

*Teri*

Teri Gay
Charlton, New York
June 2009

# PREFACE AND INTRODUCTION

**M**any books have been written about the history of the women's suffrage movement, but this one is different. The fact that it almost did not get written is perhaps one of the reasons it is not typical and also why it is not in the vain of the other histories and biographies on this topic.

It took almost thirty years to write this book. My research began as a young woman of nineteen for a 1980 winterterm history course at St. Lawrence University in Canton, New York, where I was a junior. I documented the history of the women's suffrage movement in my hometown, Glens Falls (also in New York), a topic which had long fascinated me. I was eager to read and study about suffragists in upstate New York, especially Susan B. Anthony -- who spent her girlhood years in nearby Washington County and traveled widely in this region as she worked for women's rights -- and to piece together how the suffrage fight was acted out in the area that was my home. As part of my research, I tracked down women in the greater Glens Falls area, then in their eighties and nineties, who had experienced suffrage activities – teas and lectures and meetings – to learn about female enfranchisement in the early years of the 20th century. Their descriptions about the excitement they felt – and the emotions they felt being part of a movement that carried aspects of dissent and sometimes public ridicule – brought history alive for me. Having been captivated by *national* suffrage leaders, I wanted so much to tell the story of *local* women who worked for the suffrage cause.

Inspired by respected *national* suffragists like Susan B. Anthony and Elizabeth Cady Stanton, women in locales all over America had pondered the question of the vote for women in the 19th century and early 20th century. As individuals, they searched their inner beings for the core values which would make them favorably disposed to the idea, or not, or some gradation in between. Whether or not the various categories and varied populations of women became committed to the cause of female suffrage, individual women had a complex array of considerations at work in their psyches that needed time for their reflection and decision before a commitment was made. The political identity of each woman was then, and is today, a function of many elements: her biology as a female of the species, her family and upbringing, her geography and environment, her education and intellect, her exposure to culture and ideas, her intrinsic drive for self-worth and expression through work and achievement, motherhood, marriage, personal crises and moments of character-building through adversity and challenge, the mentoring and inspiration of friendships with other women, and the psychic need for fulfilling one's potential. How women experience personal power and influence from a young age is a predictor of how they will view their world – and all their various roles in it – as the place where they can be fulfilled and can contribute. In the home, in marriage, in parenting, and in the realms of religion, education, business, and government, girls and women find their bearings through singular and personal journeys of identity development, creation of their belief systems, and their motivations for productivity in their lives.

The progression of a small female child who is dependent upon the trusted care of parents – to an adolescent girl who defines herself through the prism of family and new relationships with a larger world of peers – to an adult woman who is also perhaps a wife, a mother, or a worker, as well as a citizen of a nation – is an interlocking system of influences and complexities. As such, no two women inhabit the same psychic sphere. They are all products of the multitude of personal, familial, societal, and historical experiences that are the conditions shaping our individual places in time. The quest for personal meaning in life rises from this; likewise, the quest for identity as women in all our various roles is born out of this array of influences. And, women as participants in the political sphere – that sphere outside the domestic sphere of home and family – develop their personal constructs of believing and of behaving based on their experiences with learning about being female and the extent to which they can operate comfortably and effectively in these various roles as political beings.

My interest in the evolution of women as political contributors, participants, and leaders emanated from my 1980 college project on women's suffrage. At a time when I was evolving into the roles of womanhood that awaited me, I felt the tug to know the stories, struggles, and successes of women who had come before me. The much beloved Young Readers biographies of women I had filled the hours with as a child – Dolley Madison, Abigail Adams, Susan B. Anthony, Jane Addams, Eleanor Roosevelt – were the characters that ignited my passion for the details of strong women throughout history who had made a difference in the world and who had served as role models for girls like me.

From that jumping off point thirty years ago, I have been the wiser for the advice and lessons of these famous women I liked to read about, along with those of not-so-famous women who were family, friends, and mentors along my way. The ladies of my history books and biographies were my guides through which I learned about determination, failure, achievement, and humility. Likewise, real-life women relatives, friends, teachers, and co-workers showed me these things, and they were my examples of what it means to be a woman, to be a lady, to be feminine – and how to be a daughter, granddaughter, sister, aunt, friend, wife, mother, worker, boss, citizen – and human being. I cherish their parts in my life.

In the past thirty years of being all of these various dimensions of a woman, I have continued to research and study women's rights and suffrage, how women in different settings and regions went about organizing to win the vote, and how their personal identities and environments influenced the strategies they employed toward this goal. There was not *one* movement for suffrage. There was not a monolithic process, nor a single course that progressed in an orderly, cooperative fashion for achieving female enfranchisement nationwide in 1920, and statewide here in New York in 1917. What I learned from my study of the local, state, and national events and personalities that participated in some version of suffrage work from the 18th century through to the 20th century is that there were *many* movements within the women's suffrage movement. There were *many* competing philosophies for and against the vote for women; *many* personalities and egos which were not always in cooperative endeavor; shifting alliances among reform-minded leaders in the suffrage, abolitionist, and temperance movements; and changing rhetoric about women's suffrage that caused differences in methods and strategies for the promotion of the cause. There were dichotomies and contradictions as well.

The focus here is on the quest for political equality and suffrage as carried out by women in the small farming community of Easton, New York as set against the backdrop of suffrage work in three counties of upstate (Washington, Warren, and Saratoga) and nationwide. It tells the story of women who are not well known, whose commitment to votes for women was born not out of a feeling of being oppressed by men, but out of a philosophical belief in their natural rights as citizens of a democratic country. This is a story of women who embraced their womanliness in service to their noble cause.

These women, from their busy lives as rural farm wives, organized brilliantly to educate and inspire each other and the Easton community about the wisdom of including the female population in the voting electorate. They did not, for the most part, travel far from their small town in this endeavor nor seek the limelight of the national suffrage stage. On the contrary, they capitalized on the special brand of womanly empowerment they felt as rural ladies, operated within the comfort of their own environment, and pursued their own strategies and programs to contribute to the greater agenda of women's rights and suffrage. With support from their husbands, they convened as wives, mothers, daughters, sisters, aunts, neighbors, and friends to create an organization of political action: the Easton Political Equality Club (PEC). Through this vehicle, the ladies of the

Easton PEC became leaders in their small farming community, showing their families, friends, and neighbors – and themselves – that women are equal in citizenship and in society to men and that, together in partnership with men, democracy in the United States would be better served. You will hear them here in their own words.

As the title of this book suggests, this book about women's suffrage is specific and focused – and it offers a distinct perspective that can be seen as a model for analyzing other groups of women who cared deeply about the cause and took action on its behalf. The fight for suffrage and how it happened in the small, rural, upstate New York town of Easton at the turn of the 20th century – and which was the subject of my years of inquiry -- will now be shared with the readers of this book. What will also be shared is my belief that the secret of the success of the Easton PEC – and my personal reason for holding these ladies in high esteem – is that the formation of their political identity and impetus to political action was carried on without compromising the very essence of their femininity. They employed womanly influence in the organization of their PEC, the structure of their meetings, their message to the community, their cooperative efforts with neighboring PECs, and in their exercise of the First Amendment rights that formed the basis of their platform of pursuit of equality as an extension of their natural rights as citizens.

Through their own words (records from their meetings and in writings from the leaders), the ladies of the Easton PEC show themselves to be suffragists with their own style of feminine verve and enthusiasm. Against the backdrop of a national suffrage movement that was often fragmented and tumultuous, the suffrage work of the Easton club was unified, highly-charged, cohesive, harmonious, and done in a way which exemplified the very real positive power and influence that intrinsically female qualities engender – all at a time when women's roles were transforming in American society. The ladies of Easton were acutely aware of their evolution as women in the modern age, and their methods of working for enfranchisement revealed their hunger to improve their minds, educate each other and their families, and seek responsibility as voters and citizens for the future awaiting them in the new century. These women have captured my imagination, and I hope they will capture yours as well.

The story of the Easton PEC and its two most ardent leaders, Lucy Allen and Chloe Sisson, will be given here to honor them as models of suffrage success who did not compromise their femininity, the sanctity of their marital unions, or their families in carrying forward their work for political equality. The rhetoric and action of this rural club will be enhanced by comparisons to the active suffrage organizations in nearby Washington County communities, highlighting the effective work of Elizabeth Wakeman Mitchell in Hudson Falls and Laura Schafer Porter in Fort Edward as further examples (and no doubt there are others as well) of women who used persuasive feminine strategies in their suffrage work. A look at neighboring Warren County and two noted suffragists – Dr. Mary Putnam Jacobi and Mary Hillard Loines – will spotlight the suffrage activism of two women of wealth who also typified the model lauded in this book of blending the belief in equal rights with an emphasis on the celebration of womanliness in civic affairs. The regional perspective of this book will be rounded out with a chapter about Saratoga County's Katrina Trask, who championed women's suffrage and the concerns of the young women of regional textile mills, and who articulated these beliefs as part of her advocacy for world peace in the years of World War I.

Biographical information about these suffragists will be shared as it relates to the book's thesis. Also of note: for the purpose of using this book as a research tool and to allow the reader to focus in on an individual chapter if desired, there is a deliberate repetition of the thesis and its tangential elements throughout the book.

The thesis of this book – that women's suffrage was, in part, achieved through the earnest efforts of rural women who saw their lives as women in partnership with men and in celebration of domestic life as being ingredients for effective participation as citizen voters – will be examined through relating the story of the Easton PEC of

Washington County, New York. The ladies of Easton did not argue for their beliefs from the point of view of oppression – by their husbands, fathers, or male society – nor did they seek to emulate the platform of reformist abolitionists, many of whom were eager to wed the oppression of the black slave in white male-dominated society to the subjugation of women in 19th century America.

As a woman who grew to maturity in the 20th century (the same century in which women gained the right to vote but continue to struggle for equality on many fronts), I have often felt dismayed that the rhetoric of equal rights has been articulated in the language of oppression, particularly male oppression against women. As an outgrowth of this, it has sometimes been the case that the philosophical basis for examination of the equality of the sexes has become misconstrued. And, in an effort to reclaim power and influence, advocates for women's rights have sometimes sought to negate the separate and special qualities of men and women as a way of proving a sort of societal and sexual parity. In my own experiences as a college woman, a corporate executive, an educator, a government official, a writer, an historian, a wife, and a mother, I have often witnessed women who are willing to adopt anti-feminine, or pro-masculine, devices in their quest for equality. *What is feminine* and *what is masculine* are definitions open to many interpretations and, as I mentioned at the outset of this introduction, are very much based on personal life experiences. When I have seen girls and women achieve success and fulfill their potentials while being feminine and not seeking to negate or sublimate the very natural essence of their female selves, I have been filled with delight. To me, being a woman is the single most defining aspect of my identity as a human being. To the extent that I immerse this aura of my true self into my roles as a wife, mother, worker, or citizen, I feel I have served my inner soul to its highest and best purpose. It is my belief that when all women seek to embrace their womanliness and employ the precious qualitative gifts they possess our society and our world will be a kinder, more well-governed place. And, it will free men to also embrace the qualities of their manliness that, in combination with women's special qualities, will lead to greater understanding, peace, and equality in our world.

As we are now in the early years of the 21st century, it remains evident that the dance of delicately balancing the rights of men and women continues on. It continues in new and different ways, however. Not only is there the notion of women seeking all forms of equality in comparison to men, but there is the damaging element of *women* finding fault with *other women* – criticizing their choices about motherhood and careers, or accusing women political leaders of being unwitting pawns of partisan subterfuge. There is also the charge leveled by some feminists that other feminists are a sell-out to the cause of true equality of the sexes. Given the harsh complexity of the world for girls and young women today, it seems cruel and perverse to allow this psychological and societal onslaught of feminine fracturing to continue. Women should help, mentor, and inspire other women (and especially young girls) to become intelligent, centered, and productive human beings who are proud of their womanliness and to feel confident that their femininity will be an important ingredient in their achievement in the world. Men have a role in this, too; as fathers and husbands, brothers and uncles, they must display the support, affection, and challenge that will nurture young women toward their unique identities as adults. A world in which there is a balance and partnership between men and women, and in which women support one another in the pursuit of intellectual, human, and civic achievement, is the world for which we should all strive. In 2009, we still strive for this, as men and women alike try to cull through the messiness of life's complexities and the world's woes to be able to make sense of our respective places in it.

The musings in my head over such things for fifty years of living find a soft place to fall in the little town of Easton, at the beginning of the 20th century, with a group of women who nurtured each other and worked for female political equality – all from a spot in their feminine core. At an important moment in the history of our American democracy, they participated in a great civil rights crusade

– and succeeded with their intelligence and womanly influence.

Even today, these ladies of Easton, their indomitable spirit, and their reverence for their roles as wives, mothers, and citizens, are inspiring and moving. They are a reminder of the very best of what is inside each of us when we act in cooperative endeavor as men and women true to our distinct qualities for a better future for ourselves, our children, and the generations to come.

The story of the Easton Political Equality Club will inspire and move you as well to see the momentous possibilities when gender differences are seen as positive ingredients in societal and civic progress. Maybe this will also engender tolerance for *all* human distinctiveness – racial, ethnic, age, as well as gender – that will allow our society and our world to live in harmony and acceptance.

Let's go to Easton.

Teri Gay
Charlton, New York
June 2009

*"Let no man or woman be mistaken as to what this movement really means. We, none of us, wish to turn the world upside down, or to convert women into men. We desire women, on the contrary, above all things to continue womanly – womanly in the highest and best sense – and to bring their true women's influence, on behalf of whatsoever things are true, honest, just, pure, lovely, and of good report, to bear upon the conduct of public affairs. Lend a hand."*

Notice of a meeting of the Easton Political Equality Club in *The People's Journal*, Greenwich, New York, December 17, 1891

# Chapter I

## The Ladies of Easton:
## Womanliness, Equality, and Suffrage

The town of Easton in Washington County, in northern New York, is a place even today that seems untouched by time. The rolling hills and fertile fields that existed like a patchwork quilt in the late 1800's, when the story of the Easton Political Equality Club (PEC) begins, are as lush today, even as progress and technology industries move into the greater Capital District region, that area so named because it surrounds the state capital of Albany. From the early days of Dutch settlement in what was called New Netherland, the small, rural farming communities of upstate New York have endeavored to hold on to their colonial charm, and Easton has done that perhaps better than many others. It was the place where American primitive artist Grandma Moses (born Anna Mary Robertson in 1860) painted her enduring scenes of country life in the early 20th century. It is where the character of the residents is shaped by an idyllic array of farmland against majestic mountains and with a defining waterway, the scenic Battenkill, which rambles along on its northern boundary.

Easton's eighty square miles are tucked into the southeastern corner of Washington County, and the magnificent and historic Hudson River flows on its western side. Its sister town, Greenwich, borders it on the north, separated from it by the Battenkill, which runs through the county and which gave the towns along it an important water source for the many mills and small industries that grew up in the region during the 18th and 19th centuries. The chief business of Easton has always been agriculture – due to its advantageous soil, made of loam, clay, and sand. Even today, arable land exists to the outer reaches of every corner of the town. Streams trickle through the countryside, and the towering Willard Mountain, now a popular ski center and part of the Taghanic chain that cuts through Rensselaer and Columbia counties, serves as one of the principle reasons that regional residents know of quiet little Easton. [1]

The geography of a place is a determinant of its history. Throughout the evolution of a town – its birth, its early years as a settlement, its churnings as it transforms into what is its destiny, and how it is impacted by external forces – its character blossoms from the physical features that dictate its possibilities. This was so with Easton, and it is how, as a farming community in 1891, a group of rural women joined together to organize a political equality club, the first of its kind in Washington County – and in upstate New York.

The focus of this book will be this Easton PEC, its leaders – Lucy Allen and Chloe Sisson – and the influence it had on the cause of women's suffrage and women's rights in upstate New York at the turn of the 20th century. It will also offer a background of the women's suffrage movement nationally, a look at how political identity is formed in rural women; and, some noted suffragists of the upstate region will be introduced. The very overt feminine strategies the Easton PEC employed distinguished it from other organized suffrage groups in the state and nation. The special brand of womanly influence exhibited by the members of the Easton Club existed in contrast to many of the approaches of other suffrage advocacy groups. Often, their strategies tended to downplay or negate the essential facets of being a woman, or being a lady, in favor of more gender-neutral rhetoric. And, at times, this rhetoric characterized male society as an oppressive force which women, by proving they could be as good citizens, voters, or workers as men were, could overcome and assert their equal rights. The thesis of this book stands apart from this tendency and purports to show how brilliantly effective the PEC of rural Easton was in its participation in the women's rights movement in upstate New York by employing the very essence of its feminine gender – without compromising womanliness – for the good of the cause. It is interesting to note the contradiction of how the common device used in anti-suffragist literature and lecture appealed to what was "ladylike" about the female population to encourage a stand *against* women's suffrage. And, yet, the ladies of Easton used this same device to argue *for* female enfranchisement and to pronounce it as a constitutional right.

Here is an example of just one of the many dichotomies that existed in the women's rights movement in the 19th and early 20th centuries – and why the story of the Easton PEC needs to be told. Easton's suffrage organization represented a slightly different version of the movement, and a study of it underscores some of the basic differences between the way methods for enfranchisement varied from region to region, urban to rural, and at varying junctures at the turn of the new century. In examining the progress of women's suffrage and women's rights in America and in distinct regions of the country, it is imperative to recognize the multi-faceted aspects of the movement, its leaders, its philosophies, and its strategies. The women's suffrage (and women's rights) movement was (and is) not a singular, monolithic entity characterized by cohesive and cooperative effort on the part of its proponents and participants. The movement was, in fact, as varied as the adherents who sought to define its major thrusts and goals to a diverse American population. And, its progress over two or more centuries was affected by changing images of women as the United States evolved from a colonial farming country to an industrialized nation needing a redefinition of female labor in order to create a fully functioning society for the 20th century.

The study of women's history, therefore, is done a disservice when looked at and evaluated as being a history of sameness among women. To study Columbus and his voyages is not to understand Thomas Edison and his inventions. To examine the experience of white colonists in America does not provide a paradigm for the study of black slavery and abolition. Likewise, women's suffrage and women's rights is a panoply of diverse forces, characters, and philosophies, and the course of history has only added to the complexity of its study and understanding.

This book stands as a reminder of the variety, the distinctiveness, and the uniqueness of individual citizens – in this case, the ladies of the Easton Political Equality Club – when history is examined at its most local level.  For that is how America came to be: the pioneering spirit of individuals in small communities in the 17th and 18th centuries who worked for the dream of a nation governed by responsible citizens who would guard the rights of its people and the democratic freedoms they sought in coming here from England and Europe and elsewhere around the globe.

The examination of the Easton PEC through this prism is yet another reason to marvel at the efficacy of its efforts toward female suffrage just a century or so after the founding of America.  For Lucy Allen, Chloe Sisson, and the founding members of the PEC, the internalization of the democratic ideals they held dear and their wish to participate fully -- along with their husbands, fathers, brothers, sons, and uncles -- in the governance of their beloved community was at the very core of their identities as political beings.  They sought not to dismiss any aspect of themselves or their lives as wives, mothers, daughters, sisters, or aunts, but to utilize their womanly influence for the betterment of their rural town and the future of its generations.  While they watched and listened as women's rights lectures, writings, and speeches swirled around them in the latter part of the 19th century,  they expertly organized their own corps of women who were eager to do their own part – from the cocoon of their small Washington County town – in a drama of immense importance to American civil rights which was being played out on a statewide and a national stage.

A lot is not known about the biographies of the individual women who were the charter members of the Easton club (and the scores of other members over the years).  The written PEC meeting minutes, articles from local newspapers of the day, and the writings of its two most prominent members (Lucy Allen and Chloe Sisson), provide a glimpse into this active band of suffrage reformers.  By any standard, the effectiveness with which they organized their suffrage efforts on a local basis, and the influence they came to have on their community, county, and state, is remarkable.  They are a model of the grassroots success of individuals who see that the power and persuasion of ordinary citizens can be transforming. The ladies of Easton were not daunted by the size of their little community, being a small town of only 3,000 (at that time) residents. They were not dissuaded by the absence of legal and citizenship rights of women in 19th century society. Instead, they proclaimed themselves happy in their roles as farm wives, professed their love for their men, and went on to set up a highly effective political organization devoted to the fight for female enfranchisement in New York State and the United States. They used their bonds as family, friends, and neighbors to nurture and inspire their efforts toward this end. In so doing, they inspired and educated their community and became a model for the establishment of other political equality clubs in Washington County and the upstate region. Their courage, intelligence, and leadership in the cause of women's suffrage and women's rights (as demonstrated by the accomplishments documented in meeting minutes, letters, and news articles) shows the strength they had as individual women and as a women's group, as well as the success they achieved without compromising their lives as wives, mothers, and all manner of other feminine roles they played in their homes and in their community.

The origin of the Easton PEC in 1891 can be traced to Mary S. Anthony, younger sister of Susan B. Anthony, who is known as the grandest leader of the American suffrage movement. Both Mary and Susan, whose family lived in nearby Greenwich in the mid-1800's, had taught school as young

*Mary S. and Susan B. Anthony, 1897.*

women in and around Easton.

Writing in the early1920s, Easton PEC founding member Chloe Sisson wrote about the history of the organization in a piece that was reprinted in 1959 in a history of Washington County that included various chapters on organizations and industries of Easton and written by members of the Easton Book Club, which grew out of the PEC after its goal of votes for women was achieved statewide in 1917.[2]

In Chloe Sisson's own words:

"The Easton Political Equality Club owes a peculiar debt to Mary S. Anthony (sister of Susan B.) for it was organized and fostered through her influence throughout its early years of effort.

"[In] October 1891, a letter was received from which I quote: 'If you have no P.E.C. in your town you are just the one to call a parlor meeting of your friends and organize one, even if not more than two favor it, so that you can report to the State Convention at Auburn in November. We think it is just the time to give Woman Suffrage a boom and you will be surprised to see how easily you can do it, if you go about it right earnestly. Now, do not say no but go right ahead and you will find more than you dream of ready to work with you.'

"There was no such organization at that time in this part of the state.

"The message came like a mandate not to be disregarded. Thirty-seven years previous, in 1854, Miss Anthony was the teacher of our school for two years – one of lasting influence and throughout the succeeding years was a warm personal friend of the family where both she and her sister – Susan B. – were welcome visitors. We were early taught to respect and sympathize with their progressive ideas.

"It seemed that an effort must be made to comply with this request, although very few were known that would favor such a movement. Upon consulting with these, so much encouragement was received that a meeting was called of which I will read the minutes in part: 'At the solicitation of Mary S. Anthony, Secretary of the State Woman

Suffrage Association, a meeting was duly called at Marshall Seminary, on October 10, 1891, for the purpose of organizing a Political Equality Club. Ten women responded to the call. A paper was read giving a brief review of the Woman Suffrage Association and outlining the proposed work of a Political Equality Club. The constitution prepared by the state association was read and adopted by eight of those present. ' Officers were elected and the meeting adjourned to October 24, when five additional members were received, and a delegate appointed to attend the State Convention in November, when our membership had increased to twenty.

"After our club was fairly launched the meetings were held monthly, as now and for some time Miss Anthony sent material, suggestions and encouragement, for each meeting, and had never lost interest in it. We find in looking over the minutes that the most strenuous part of its work was done under her leadership during the first few years of its history. Even that done in the name of the county club was then performed largely by the Easton Club and in many cases wholly so.

"The following winter Miss Anthony sent us an account of the first Woman's Day at the State Fair, and some of the County Fairs, under the auspices of the suffragists – and urged us to try to have one at our County Fair with a good speaker recommending Rev. Anna Howard Shaw [President of the National American Woman Suffrage Association 1904 – 1915], then a stranger to us. Accordingly, a committee was appointed to attend the meeting of the Directors of the Cambridge [neighboring town] Fair in March, and prove to them from its financial success at others' fairs that it would be a profitable investment to make a Woman's Day one of the special attractions – also of the fame and ability of the speaker. Two months later the committee was informed that, with difficulty, the Directors were induced to comply with our request.

"We found it quite an undertaking for a few inexperienced women. However, we went to work with a will, had several meetings to complete the arrangements, and much work was done at the homes of the members, as well as on the fairgrounds.

*PEC Carriage, 1892.*

"From the minutes of the first annual meeting I find we had thirty paid-up members, raised and expended $29.00; secured a Woman's Day at the Cambridge Fair, for which we made eight large mottoes, an equal rights banner and the fields for two Wyoming flags – Wyoming then being the only state where women voted on the same terms as men – decorated a carriage to represent our club in the Floral Parade; arranged for fifteen lectures in twelve towns, which were given by the state organizer, Miss Cheney; obtained seventy subscribers to the suffrage papers; distributed a large amount of suffrage literature; purchased two books for the use of the club; supplied a column in one weekly paper and contributed several articles to others; secured the establishment of the first Franchise department in the county W.C.T.U. [Women's Christian Temperance Union], and had a discussion of the question in each of the fourteen local unions, three of which appointed Franchise Superintendents. One social was held.

"At this time the State Suffrage Association was already preparing for a campaign asking to have the word 'male' stricken out of the constitution of our state at the approaching Constitutional Convention held in 1894.

"In the summer of 1893 although engaged in enrolling petitions to this Convention as was being done throughout the state, we were also endeavoring to inform the women of our election district of their right to vote for school commissioner at the coming election, and of their duty to exercise it, from an act passed by the Legislature of 1892.

"While employed in this work we interested Mrs. Hubbard and Mrs. Stoddard of Cambridge. With the aid of the state organizer, Miss Harriet May Mills, a club was organized there, and also one at Shushan [a neighboring town]. The political parties had already nominated their candidates when we were advised by the state association to nominate a woman as an independent candidate. Some other counties were doing so. Accordingly a convention of the County Political Equality Clubs was called in Easton, and Mrs. Alice Stoddard [was] nominated as our candidate for School Commissioner.

"We had circulars scattered broadcast, setting forth the superior qualifications of Mrs. Stoddard, the advantages of women as school officers, and the importance of this office being taken out of partisan politics. At the outset we had little hope of anything more than getting women to exercise their privilege of registering and voting. After most of the leading politicians had been personally interviewed and their support promised, Mrs. Stoddard, at least, had considerable hope of being elected. We cannot recall the number of votes she received, but know she did make quite a credible showing. The action of women in voting for School Commissioner was that fall declared by several judges of the Supreme Court to be unconstitutional.

"Before the Constitutional Convention convened in Albany, 600,000 names of the adult men and women of the state had been enrolled on the petitions. A two day's mass meeting had been held during the previous winter and spring in each of the sixty counties with two prominent speakers for each day. BESIDE THE LOCAL TALENT ENLISTED, SUSAN B. ANTHONY SPOKE ONE DAY, OR EVENING, IN EACH COUNTY MEETING. SHE WAS THEN PAST SEVENTY YEARS OF AGE.

"Our part in the work is reported as follows: The Cambridge and

Easton Clubs made the arrangements for the mass meeting at Cambridge, Feb. 8 – 9, 1894, which was a phenomenal success. One hundred fourteen dollars was raised there for the campaign. Mr. Hobby, then assemblyman, and Mr. McArthur of Granville [in northeastern Washington County] came up from Albany to make addresses for us. Chairmen were appointed in each town of Washington County. The total number of signatures obtained to the petition was 3,500. A complete list of the taxpaying women of the county with the assessed valuation of each was made. Personal letters were sent to each of the hundred-seventy-five delegates of the Constitutional Convention, and others were repeatedly sent to its delegates from our district. We are proud to say that Frederick Fraser, of Salem [adjacent to Cambridge], and Charles H. Moore, of Plattsburg [in northern New York] were of the number who voted for the amendment. Our plea [to have the word 'male' stricken from the state constitution] was voted down by ninety-seven men found ready to sacrifice principle to party.

"No more pathetic stories are told of the struggle for liberty in the old days of the Revolution than are told of the women of New York State in that campaign.

"In 1897 we purchased material and made our suffrage flag. The four yellow stars representing the four equal suffrage states – Wyoming, Colorado, Utah, and Idaho.

"In December 1900 we obtained twenty-five subscribers to the Woman's Journal [a publication of the American Woman Suffrage Association, starting in 1870] and received the premium of twenty dollars cash for our treasury.

"The next undertaking of our club of which I have record, other than our regular work, was that for the National Suffrage Bazaar, held in Madison Square Garden in New York in December 1901 to raise funds to carry on the National work. During the previous summer and fall our members made articles for it, (including the ten rag dolls), valued at a hundred dollars.

"During the most severe weather of a cold, snowy winter meetings were arranged for Miss Mills in several towns when she organized the White Creek, Granville, and West Hebron [all towns in Washington County] Clubs, and addressed the Farmers' Institute at Valley Falls [neighboring Easton, in Rensselaer County].

" In 1910 a delegation from our club was invited to organize the North Easton Study Club, which has proved a strong ally and prompts us to look well to our laurels.

"In those earlier years we had more frequent public meetings, lectures and entertainments, [and] most of the county conventions were held at Easton. With one exception we always sent one or more delegates to the State Convention. Mrs. Hubbard of Cambridge represented our county at the National Convention at Washington [D.C.] so long as she was able to make the journey. She contributed liberally to the cause.

"The average number of members has been kept good for all the many depletions by removals and death.

"If our younger members will take up the work, as they now promise to do, with ever increasing zeal, inspired by the faith that woman suffrage is the lever that underlies every other reform, and that 'Failure is Impossible' [Susan B. Anthony's rallying slogan], the Washington County Club will be counted when the Victory is won, and will receive the blessings of 'Well Done.' Let us resolve to make the coming year more fruitful than any that lie [behind us].

"Deserving of further mention is the contribution of the Easton Club in the preparation for the great National Suffrage Bazaar, held in Madison Square Garden in New York, in December 1901, to which every club was asked to donate articles for sale. The members valiantly undertook an ambitious program of fund raising. Three successful efforts in this line served not only to bring in money, but to arouse interest, increase membership, and to add the spice of fun that come when all work together unselfishly for a worthy cause.

"Inspired by Emily Peckham – sister of Chloe A. Sisson [the author of this] – the Easton Club members made ten most wonderful rag dolls – the queens of all dolldom. They were about the size of a year old child. The removable clothes were exquisitely handmade of finest materials with dainty embroidery. Tiny buttonholes were works of art. Emily Peckham drew and painted the faces. The eyebrows were embroidered, also the hair. Some were blondes, some brunettes. The finished dolls made such a brave display, the ladies were loath to part with them; but they made a sensation at the Bazaar, and sold like hot cakes for ten dollars each. Nothing like them was on display. Many more could have been sold, but the one-hundred dollars they did bring was a creditable amount from such a small club. Easton received many compliments for this effort and special thanks from Susan B. Anthony herself. The club received from her as a gift the 1144 page volume IV of The History of Woman Suffrage. It bears on the flyleaf this inscription:

'To Mrs. Lucy P. Allen;

This huge Volume IV is presented to your Political Equality Club because of its contribution [in 1901] to the proposed Standing Fund and for your cheerful consent to its transference to the printing of this book.

Sincerely and Affectionately,
Susan B. Anthony
Rochester, N.Y. '

"The great National Suffrage Bazaar netted $8,000 for the association.

"The next fund raising activity of the Easton Club, which meant long hours of hard work for all the nearby members – those at greater distance helping with cash donations – was the opening of a Suffrage Headquarters at Aaron B. Allen's vacant store building at Barker's Grove [a hamlet in south Easton]. The preparation of this old building was an herculean task. All the shelving, the walls, and the ceiling were smoke grimed, fly-specked, and dirty – to say nothing of the tobacco spitting area around the spot where the stove had been. Members cleaned and cleaned, and polished until all was neat, attractive, and shining.

"Then came the decoration to which Mary S. Taylor, assisted by Mary A. Eddy, devoted her time and her artistic ability. Large amounts of yellow and white [the suffrage colors] crepe paper were used. All the shelves were covered with white, edged with narrow ruffled bands of yellow. A canopy of streamers, alternating the two columns went from the center of the ceiling to the sides. At the back hung the large suffrage flag with yellow silk fringe, the stars of the suffrage states embroidered in yellow, more of the exquisite needlework done by Emily Peckham. Over the flag, arranged in an arch, letters of gold spelled Easton Political Equality Club. This made a brave display. Mary M. Phillips, Lucy Allen's mother, cut the large letters from stiff cardboard, then covered them with gilt paper, a painstaking task of devotion. In the front windows and on the walls were attractive posters and pictures of suffrage leaders. Along one side of the room the counter was kept well-stocked with suffrage literature; along the other was the food donated for sale. Ice cream and cake were furnished by the members. Mary Wicks made the ice cream, sending her two little colored boys [Chloe's own words] up to Mrs. Allen's for 'as much Jersey cream as she could spare.' The beautiful cakes, examples of the skill and artistry of Easton cooks, were often brought on foot by those who made them.

"Members took turns being always on hand to expound the Suffrage Cause and dip the ice cream, Sunday afternoons and evenings were the most lucrative times. Then the young courtin' couples in their fancy rigs came to eat cake and ice cream, but preferred to have it served outside – thus antedating the curb-service of modern days.

"This effort, providing too much of a strain for all concerned, was discontinued after one season.

"Another undertaking, which earned funds and praise for the club, was the presentation at Burton Hall [today's Town Hall] of the three-act drama, 'The Blue and the Grey' directed by Lucy P. Allen. Since it was before the days of automobiles, transportation of the cast for rehearsals was an ever present difficulty.  In spite of all setbacks, however, the final production was most successful.

"Other plays and entertainments followed.   There was a large attendance at an outdoor social at the home of Mrs. [and] Dr. Elmer Mosher.  A platform was built on the lawn for the presentation of the operetta, 'King Alfred,' and for 'Getting the Ruggles Family Ready for Christmas Dinner,' and for 'The Birds' Christmas Carol.'

"The regular work of the club continued.   Outstanding women [suffragists] were invited to lecture at Burton Hall.  Among them were Alice Duer Miller, Harriet May Mills, Mrs. Fenwick Miller, an English woman, who was one of the delegates to the Washington [D.C.] Suffrage Convention, and most beloved of all – the Rev. Anna Howard Shaw.  All gave stirring, eloquent speeches, which helped materially to create a favorable sentiment in the community.

"Some of these lectures were given in the winter when travel conditions were difficult.  In horse and buggy days it was not easy to meet trains, and arrange entertainment.  The visiting speakers also endured much hardship in the way of inconvenient travel, for their faith.  I remember that Dr. Shaw had just suffered an accident.  Both her hands, having been severely burned, were heavily bandaged.  She was an elderly, white haired woman, who might easily have stayed at home to nurse her hurts.  But, as always, the spirit of our pioneer leaders rose triumphant over the ills of the flesh.  The CAUSE came first.  Nothing else mattered.

" So it went on, the supreme effort of these devoted women to win the right of suffrage.   Easton sent delegates to help organize two neighboring clubs.

" Rev. Anna Howard Shaw with Harriet May Mills organized on May 13, 1903 a club at Valley Falls.  At the first meeting held at the Baptist Church, Mrs. Lucy Thompson was elected its first president.  She was soon succeeded by Mrs. Blanche Clum, who proved an ardent leader.  This club, now the Valley Falls Woman's Club, is a large and influential group of women.

"A second club was organized in 1901 at North Easton of which Fanny Conklin was leader. Both of these groups were sister clubs, helpful and enthusiastic in every united undertaking for the cause. Of the other clubs Cambridge was organized in 1893, then Shushan. It was in 1901 or 1902 that clubs were organized in White Creek, Granville, and West Hebron. Thus Easton spread its influence over a wide area.

" Lucy P. Allen was president of the local club during its most active years, then president of the Washington County Branch of the New York State Woman Suffrage Party.

"Local meetings were held once each month in the homes of the members. A yearbook, dated 1917 – 1918, bears the motto – 'For God, For Home, For Every Land.' Roll call was responded to by current events. Programs were varied. In addition to book reviews and selected topics a series of Bible studies was given. Shakespeare plays were read aloud, each member taking a part. Miss Mary Sprague, a cultured gentlewoman of the old school, read delightfully from Dickens, her favorite and loved author. Those who heard her could never forget her keen enjoyment of his characters.

"Thus the club continued, an intellectual and a social activity for its members, always with some money raising effort being carried on to advance the cause of suffrage. After the great victory was won by the passing of the nineteenth amendment giving all women the franchise [in 1920], the club – its goal having been accomplished – was reluctantly disbanded." [3]

" Oct. 19, 1891 – The Ten Original Members of the Easton PEC:

1.  Lucy P. Allen
2.  Emma Skiff Becker
3.  Mary A. Eddy
4.  Emily E. Peckham
5.  Addie W. Perry
6.  Mary M. Phillips
7.  Chloe A. Sisson

8.  Anna M. Stiles
9.  Mary S. Taylor
10. Fannie D. Thompson

"Oct. 24, 1891 - At the second meeting of the club five new members were added:

Lydia G. Batty
Nellie C. Batty
Anna F. Frisbie
Lydia Dwelle Hoag
Celestia Allen Slocum

"Later Members:

Frank Baker
Alice S. Becker – Mrs. Lester J.
Louise Charbono (Benson) – Mrs. Harry
Anna T. Brown – Mrs. Edgar
Gertrude W. Brownell – Mrs. George H.
Josephine E. Brownell – Mrs. Thomas
Alma J. Case – Mrs. Charles
Sarah Conklin – Mrs. Edward
Phebe Phillips Deuel – Mrs. George
Cena Brown Dixon – Mrs. William
Elizabeth Hoag – Mrs. Isaac
Phebe A. Hoag – Daughter of Isaac
Azetta Kipp – Mrs. Cornelius
Etta Almy Lawrence – Mrs. Albert
Clara Henderson (Mulligan) – Mrs. William
Anna B. Allen (Pratt) – Mrs. Jacob F.
Mabel Charbono (Ryan) – Mrs. William
Hetty Snell – Mrs. Warren E.
Sophia F. Sisson – Mrs. Burton L."[4]

Chloe Sisson was a delegate to the first Republican state convention following the passage of the Nineteenth Amendment in 1920 granting women the right to vote in the United States. She had the distinction of being the first woman from Washington County to attend a New York State political convention.[5]

An examination of the Easton PEC through the writings of its leaders, minutes of its meetings, and newspaper accounts of its activities will be highlighted in this book, along with the premise that Easton's suffrage work and the political identities of its leaders and members were shaped and enhanced by use of their womanliness. This book will offer information gleaned through research of the above materials, and interpreted by considering the place and point in time of this small suffrage organization. The story of the Easton club exists mid-stream in the mainstream women's suffrage movement, starting in the 1890's and ending shortly after suffrage was achieved in 1920. No esoteric theories are presented here – just the charming story of a small but industrious group of rural farm women who worked for the achievement of equal rights within the context of their domestic sphere. Motivated by an underlying belief in the democratic ideas of the Founding Fathers and a desire to preserve and protect the sacred life they had built in a town they dearly loved and on land which was their livelihood, they achieved something great.

Some biographical information, where it is available, will be offered in the upcoming chapters as it relates to the book's thesis, but this is not as much a book of biographies of the Easton ladies (or the other suffragists from neighboring counties that will be profiled) as it is an account of collective action for a greater good by women who did it their way. Their story fits into the patchwork of regional women's rights history, along with other noted suffragists of nearby communities which will be presented in a manner which shows their interconnectedness, and which offers contrasts to the plethora of strategies and methods used by various suffrage leaders and groups in the 19th and early 20th centuries in the United States.

It is a tale of friendship and sisterhood, geography and attachment to the land, citizenship and humanity. How the women of the Easton PEC influenced (and were influenced by) the greater statewide and national suffrage movement will no doubt engender more questions which cannot all be answered here. This study will delight in the remarkable ability of women who lived in small town rural America to internalize their intellectual understanding of democratic citizenship and to take action for a cause that was, from the early days of our nation, too shocking and too unladylike – in the opinions of some – to even be considered.

Amidst the competing philosophies and paths to suffrage tried by various factions involved in the women's suffrage movement, the ladies of Easton embraced the very basic elements of their lives – family, motherhood, rural life, farming, religion, and the domestic arts – and put them to work for the cause. To these core institutions, they added an intellectual component and, through their PEC meetings, educated and nurtured one another on a wide-ranging array of literary, scientific, philosophical, and civic topics, making them truly women of the modern era.  Through their earnest endeavors, they participated in the progress of women as citizens who, through the power of the vote, could influence and determine the future of their community, their state, and their nation.  From rural Easton, these ladies showed themselves to be ready to join in sisterhood with women of all categories who struggled for equality – rural and urban women, working women, factory girls, immigrant women – as the 20th century loomed.  They organized and sprang into action at a pivotal point in time and displayed an incredible degree of camaraderie and unity with other suffrage clubs and groups in their region and beyond.  Poised for action as the new century began, the Easton PEC exhibited extraordinary strength of resolve.  For a group of its small size, it had enormous influence, and its leaders – Lucy Allen and Chloe Sisson – gained notoriety for their articulate and eloquent writings and speeches on behalf of suffrage in upstate New York.

History too often focuses on the *famous few* who leave a big mark on the world because they are widely known or do things that attract national or international prominence.  Hidden among the many others in the world, however, are the *extraordinary ordinary* who do great things in the course of their private, not well-known, lives, but which, nevertheless, count heavily in the betterment of humankind. It is just this wrinkle of history that drives the need to uncover and relate the heroic sagas of those who have changed life for the better in places we may never have heard of – or places we call home.  From this wellspring of attachment to our environs and the people, past and present, who have inhabited that space with us and thereby share our history, we learn and appreciate why and how historical progress happened this way here.

The way that the ladies of Easton demonstrated their allegiance to the cause of women's suffrage was a by-product of their own attachment to Easton, their farming way-of-life, their lives as rural women, and their hunger for intellectual stimulation and growth. In any type of history – of a nation, of a people, or of a cause – is it not the case that history is often made by the intersection of individual motivation with the collective embrace of an idea which is novel or controversial?

So it was in Washington County, New York in 1891, in the midst of a national women's suffrage fight, that the Easton Political Equality Club emerged as an energetic player in what was to become one of the greatest struggles in American civil rights history.

# Chapter II
## The Origins of the Women's Suffrage Movement in Upstate New York and America

In 1891, when the Easton Political Equality Club (PEC) was being formed, the national women's suffrage movement was undergoing a massive reorganization. Decades of trying to articulate a cogent ideology and agenda for action that would resonate with the states and all their regional differences, and with the nation, to win the female franchise had been marked by struggle, competing strategies, shaky coalitions with other reformist groups, and clashing personalities. The passing over of women as voters after the Civil War amendments (Thirteen, Fourteen, and Fifteenth) left the suffrage movement soured, jaded, and in chaos.

The fracture caused by the failure to garner support for a federal amendment granting the vote to women, however, may have in fact been just the spark to ignite a new spirit of cooperation among the corps of national suffrage leaders and help define a true and standalone *women's suffrage movement* which was not a tangential piece of temperance or abolition, but a cause all its own.

As a result, in 1890, the National Woman Suffrage Association (NWSA), led by Susan B. Anthony and Elizabeth Cady Stanton, and the American Woman Suffrage Association (AWSA), led by Lucy Stone, merged into the National American Woman Suffrage Association (NAWSA), with Stanton at the helm. Alice Stone Blackwell, daughter of Lucy Stone and reformer Henry Blackwell, facilitated the coming-together of the two rival organizations. NWSA, centered in New York State, had had a radical reaction to the dismissal of women's suffrage after the Civil War and had refused to help with the ratification of the Fifteenth Amendment enfranchising blacks. It sought instead an amendment (the *Sixteenth*, supposedly) to grant *universal* suffrage – male and female, black and white and without restriction due to race.  AWSA, on the other hand, working out of Boston, did not try to work against the passage of the Civil War amendments and supported the coalition of suffrage and anti-slavery leaders.[1]

Reconfigured, therefore, after 1890, the women's suffrage movement gained a new momentum, a more unified focus, and a belief in working state-by-state across the Union to fight for voting rights for women.  The push for more regional and local women's suffrage organizations was born out of this critical time period and is what surely led to the establishment of the Easton PEC (among other clubs in upstate New York), whose creation was given a little shove by the motivational letter from Susan B. Anthony's younger sister, Mary Stafford Anthony, a noted suffragist in her own right.

Whether or not women's suffrage was a major topic of discussion or controversy in Easton prior to 1891 is a matter of speculation, but it appears it surely was.  And, the mere fact of the PEC's strong origin, effective organization, and prepared leaders suggests a community ripe for suffrage work and one for whom the issue was well known.

From the founding of America in 1776, rumblings of discontent among women, who recognized their inferior status vis à vis men in a land purportedly founded on democratic and egalitarian ideals and who were willing to defy public outcry and condemn the irony of it, were evident.  The fight for the franchise was actually part and parcel of a larger agenda of feminist reform that had its antecedents in 17th and 18th century England and America.  English Common Law, on which American laws were based, held women at a status equal to that of minors and held that women were inferior physically and mentally to men.  Unmarried women existed under the control of their fathers or uncles; married women were subject to the control of their husbands.  Women could not own property; all their possessions passed into ownership of their spouses upon marriage.  They had no rights to their own children in the event of divorce.[2]

At the time of the American colonies' meeting in 1776 to assert their independence from England and start a revolution, Abigail Adams, wife of John Adams (who would become the nation's second President), wrote to her husband on behalf of women, with this now famous phrase: *Remember the ladies*. The resulting Declaration of Independence, however, read: *All men are created equal*, setting the stage for the wording in the Declaration of Sentiments, the document which resulted from the first women's rights convention, held in Seneca Falls, New York in 1848. The women's declaration proclaimed: "*All men and women are created equal*," and officially started a revolution of another kind – the revolution for women's rights and suffrage. [3]

From the early 1800s, published books, journals, literary works, and letters reveal that the topics of womens rights, education, and the female franchise were being debated across the nation by members of both sexes. Women, in particular, were seeking forums to discuss and express the conditions of their separate, domestic sphere, a phenomenon which came to be called the *cult of domesticity*. By about 1820, the connection between women's lack of legal standing and the necessity for voting rights to rectify that became more evident in the writings and speeches of women's rights advocates and reformers. [4]

A push for equal education for girls and young women accompanied this. In 1821, Emma Willard opened the all-girls Troy Female Seminary in Troy, New York. Suffrage leader Elizabeth Cady Stanton, who was from Johnstown in Fulton County, attended the school between 1831 and 1833. Oberlin College opened its doors to women in 1833, becoming the first coeducational institution of higher learning in America. Suffragists Lucy Stone and Antoinette Brown were among its first graduates. Mary Lyon founded the first female four-year college, Mount Holyoke in Holyoke, Massachusetts. Other colleges founded in this period as all-female places of higher education were: Vassar College (1861), Wellesley College (1875), and Smith College (1875). [5] Clearly, women sought freedom to be educated in amongst other social and political forms of emancipation.

A review of suffrage ideology from the early 19th century reveals a changing body of rhetoric which reflected individual beliefs, religious influences, geography, and well-formed coalitions within the various reformist movements. Early British feminist and writer Mary Wollstonecraft, author of *A Vindication of the Rights of Woman*, published in 1792, put forth her theories of women's rights by exposing misogynist views of women as reasons for female weaknesses and feelings of inferiority which were then perpetrated by men *against women*. Wollstonecraft, however, was among the first women's rights theorists to advance the notion of *reason* (the idea that human beings are rational creatures governed by rationality) as the basis upon which rights for women should be granted.[6]

By the time that well known women's rights leaders Susan B. Anthony, Elizabeth Cady Stanton, Lucretia Mott, and Lucy Stone were organizing a cogent response to the debate over women's place in male-dominated 19th century society, reformist sentiment was growing in America. The evils of alcohol were becoming exposed as a major ill of society, and temperance organizations on the local and national levels were being created. Anti-slavery sentiment was also growing, as the concept of enslavement of blacks by whites was considered unjust and immoral. Abolitionist groups and the formation of an "underground railroad" network to aid fugitive slaves became an early example of the effective coalition of white and black activists who sought to eradicate the oppression of blacks in America. New York, in fact, which had been one of the largest slaveholding states in the years following the American Revolution, abolished slavery in 1827 – just at the time that articulation of women's rights and suffrage was gaining sophistication. Nationally, regionally, and in New York state, women exercised their first attempts at being leaders in reform activity through temperance and anti-slavery societies – experience which was later to serve them well as their own women's suffrage fight took off.

The Second Great Awakening in America (beginning about 1837) and its philosophical prophet Reverend Charles Finney signaled a renaissance of the morality of humankind and led to a renewed consciousness of benevolence, charity, and religious fervor. This period and its prevailing attitude were born out of New England Congregationalism and aided 19th century reformist causes. Again, regionally in New York, this revivalism ignited reformist sentiments for temperance, abolition, and suffrage, causing the central area of the state – from whence hailed many of the most well-known reformers – to be called "the burned-over district" for its reputation as the area through which the fires of reform were raging. The preponderance of egalitarian belief and a reform-minded population carried over to the upstate, northern New York region as well – to Quaker communities in Glens Falls (Warren County), Quaker Springs (Saratoga County), and Easton (Washington County), and also to Baptist communities in Saratoga County.

The Civil War (1861 – 1865) brought cataclysmic changes to America, decimating the male population in cities and towns in the North and South, exposing the racial divide, and pushing a weakened national economy toward industrialization. The national suffrage movement, led by Anthony and Stanton, took a hiatus from its activities during the war years and joined forces with anti-slavery leaders like Frederick Douglass, Sojourner Truth, and sisters Sarah and Angelina Grimké to work for an end to slavery – hoping that their selfless efforts would be rewarded by the passage of a federal amendment granting universal suffrage. When this did not result, and the Thirteen, Fourteenth, and Fifteenth Amendments were passed – giving blacks *freedom, citizenship, and the vote* – there began a period of backlash and fracture in the women's suffrage movement.

By 1870, intrepid leaders Anthony and Stanton had turned against the Republican administration – and many anti-slavery leaders – to join together with certain Democratic Party figures (George Francis Train, in particular) who opposed the policies of Reconstruction. Shocked and dismayed at being passed over after having put aside their own suffrage agenda for abolition, Anthony and Stanton and their followers embarked upon a campaign of racist attack against the new black citizens they had previously sought to empower. Their vitriolic attacks extended to Native Americans, as well as to the influx of ethnic groups immigrating to the United States, whom they viewed as less intelligent than American-born white women, and not deserving of legal protections or the right to vote – all of which were still withheld from the white female population.

This was among the first clues that the voice of the national women's suffrage movement was shaped by middle- and upper-class white women who articulated an agenda for winning the franchise that was not only *gender* – driven, but *class* – driven, and *ethnically*- and *racially*-biased. It was not until the early 20th century, when the state-by-state strategy for winning the vote was deemed a failure and a decision was made by NAWSA leader Carrie Chapman Catt to focus on the "Winning Plan" for a federal amendment, did class, racial, and ethnic barriers start to tumble.

Condescending attitudes of middle- and upper-class women's suffrage leaders changed and became more inclusive when coalitions with lower-class, working women of the northeast United States and black women across the country were formed and a unified path forward for suffrage was established. By the 1910's, mutual respect on all sides by women's rights advocates eventually made the difference in being able to begin to end generations of legal, economic, social, and political inequality for women in America.

Geography played an important role, too; as suffrage activists struggled in the eastern United States, western states and territories led the way in granting the vote to their female populations. Aided by egalitarian attitudes, a pioneering way of life, and the necessity of solid male-female partnerships in the settling of the West,  these states and territories gave unrestricted voting rights to women: Wyoming (in 1869), Utah (in 1870), Washington (in 1883), Alaska and Kansas (in 1912),  and Nevada and Montana (in 1914).

New York State became the first eastern state to fully enfranchise women in 1917. As seen against the backdrop of suffrage and 19th century reformist movements across the United States, women's rights activities – including those in rural upstate New York – reflect the influence of national personalities on local and regional participation in women's suffrage, temperance, and abolition.

When New Yorkers gave women the right to vote on November 6, 1917, the people of the upstate counties of Washington, Warren, and Saratoga felt a sense of pride. This milestone of feminist reform had been achieved in part thanks to the efforts of dynamic individuals with ties to this rural upstate region as well as to the tireless work of powerful local suffrage organizations, like the Easton PEC. In an environment characterized by progressive ideas – rooted in Protestant, Baptist, and Quaker religious ideology, rural traditions, fervent temperance activity, and abolitionist sentiment – women's suffrage was a lively issue in the region in the century preceding the passage of the state amendment.

Central New York, however, had been the birthplace of suffrage reform. The women's right's convention held in Seneca Falls in 1848 had sought to radically change the conditions of women all across America in the 19th century. The forward-thinking women (and a few men) who gathered there set out to correct the social, economic, legal, and political subjugation of women. Reverberations rippled out across the state and the country, and over the next seventy-two years the fight for suffrage was waged in every corner of America. New York was a central stage for much of this activity. In fact, all the women's right conventions between 1850 and 1858 were held in New York State, underscoring the influence of native sons and daughters who led the suffrage charge.  Some additional, but still small, steps toward greater legal rights for women were being taken in the state in the second half of the century–namely, the Married Women's Property Act of 1848, which gave women the right to control property they possessed at the time of marriage or which they inherited during marriage; and the Earnings Act of 1860, which gave married women the right to control their own earnings, joint legal custody of minor children, and the right to sue in a court of law.

By the second half of the 19th century, large national organizations had formed to fight state-by-state for the vote.  Believing that a broader array of equal rights could be gained by guaranteeing the franchise for women, feminist reform advocates focused firmly on winning *the vote* over other rights. However, they saw the necessity of forming alliances at various junctures – with temperance societies, anti-slavery groups – even labor unions – sometimes out of expediency, but, for the most part, out of a shared commitment to the morally-based domestic reform that characterized this period in American history. [7]

Through their emerging leadership roles in reform societies, women had sharpened their political skills on the tactics and strategies of developing their own major civil rights movement. It was through these early activities, and eventually through their suffrage campaign, that women learned how to organize, how to speak in public, how to exercise their right of assembly, how to petition the government, and how to picket for their cause. Suffragists endured decades of criticism, ostracism, and even violence in their quest for justice and equality. What was even more perplexing and frustrating was that much of the opposition they encountered came from other women. Suffrage was a divisive and emotionally-charged issue. [8]

The "cult of womanhood" that had kept women in a separate sphere through the early 20th century had its beginnings in pre-Revolutionary War America, when motherhood and patriotism were inextricably linked. Coming to a pinnacle in the Victorian era, womanhood was associated with quiet virtue, morality, and a family-centered life. In service to this paternalistic ideal, women were kept protected from the rough and tumble of "dirty politics" by a male-dominated society. In fact, it was believed that women could wield *greater* power and influence by *not* voting – that their superior moral instincts should naturally lead them into the arenas of benevolent societies, church work, and volunteerism, using those avenues to further the improvement of home and community. This argument, by the way, was one of many used rather effectively by the anti-suffragists in their campaign against female suffrage. However, the Victorian era also witnessed rumblings of discontent among a new generation of women who wanted access to higher education, careers in addition to motherhood, and more independent lives. Indeed, the changing roles for women, in addition to the fight for suffrage, put women at odds with each other as well as with men as the cause grew to a crescendo in the first two decades of the 20th century.[9]

While cataclysmic events were playing out around the county, the rural upstate New York region was experiencing its own buzz of feminist activity. Perhaps one beneficial factor contributing to active regional support was the influence of Quakers. Quaker religious belief valued equal education for men and women and equality between the sexes. The city of Glens Falls in Warren County was founded by Quakers. Quaker Springs in Saratoga County was a place of long-held Friends tradition. The town of Easton (the focus of this book) in Washington County likewise had a strong Quaker community which had progressive leanings. The Easton Political Equality Club was founded with the great assistance of a very devout Quaker, Mary S. Anthony, whose family were Hicksite Quakers, a liberal wing of the faith. [10]

The example of the Easton PEC and its two devoted leaders, Lucy Allen and Chloe Sisson, typified the local brand of suffrage activity which reflected the unique characteristics of rural upstate communities in and around the foothills of the Adirondack Mountains. This small club heartily motivated women throughout Easton, Greenwich, Fort Edward, Hudson Falls, Washington County, and the surrounding area to work with them to gain support for suffrage. The Easton PEC formed strong alliances with state and national suffrage organizations and aided them in fundraising. It was the model of a local club whose intense commitment to equality resonated soundly in an agricultural region where women worked alongside men and shared in equal ways the burdens and rewards of farming life. It was perhaps this hearty, pioneering spirit – which was also present in the rugged, individualistic folk of the Adirondack Mountains region – that fostered an egalitarian stance that cut across gender lines to encourage support for the cause of suffrage in upstate. [11]

Temperance and suffrage organizations were often mutually supportive, both nationally and in upstate New York. The vision of an ax-wielding Carrie Nation was a symbol of the evils of liquor, a cause that thousands of women across America and in England united to win. The nation's first temperance society, and all-male – The Moreau and Northumberland Temperance Society – was founded in Moreau, Saratoga County in 1808 by Dr. Billy Clark. This society earned high acclaim and drew nationally known reformers to the area, which benefitted both the temperance *and* suffrage movements.[12]

A case in point to provide evidence of the symbiotic relationship between temperance and suffrage: a men's temperance convention was held in Saratoga Springs in 1854. Susan B. Anthony, with long ties to the area and with her strong Quaker conviction about temperance, decided to hold her own conference in the resort city – to give women a voice in matters of prohibition and women's rights. This was one of Anthony's many efforts in upstate New York to connect feminist, religious, and reformist causes and to rally women in a united campaign. By 1874, the national Women's Christian Temperance Union (WCTU) was established; in 1876, its most famous leader, Frances E. Willard, was at the helm, and a partnership with women's suffrage ensued. Frances Willard, in fact, used the phrase "womanly influence" in speaking about the positive effect of women on societal reform. [13]

Connections between the religious underpinnings of the temperance movement and abolitionist activity also aided the suffrage cause. In rural upstate New York, sympathies for all three movements were strong. Two temperance societies flourished in Warren County – the Central Women's Christian Temperance Union, formed in 1885 by Alice Boyd, and the Mission Women's Christian Temperance Union, formed in 1888 – both in Glens Falls. Anti-slavery sentiment manifested itself in an active "underground railroad" throughout Warren, Washington, and Saratoga counties and northward into Canada. The population of the southern Adirondack region at the turn of the 20th century was immersed in these controversial issues of the day. [14]

This is not to suggest that the leaders and participants in these sometimes overlapping reformist movements saw things completely compatibly at all times. Not so. As mentioned earlier, the aims and strategies of these groups sometimes coincided nicely, and alliances were fruitful. Sometimes, however, collaborations broke down, personalities clashed, and goals were thwarted. A case in point was the racist rhetoric of many suffrage leaders following the passage of the Fifteenth Amendment, born out of resentment at having been overlooked for equal suffrage in favor of black men. Likewise, when abolitionist Gerrit Smith (cousin of suffragist Elizabeth Cady Stanton) attempted to settle freed black slaves in the Adirondacks following the Civil War, his initiatives did not go over well with some North County-based suffrage groups. [15]

The stature of Susan B. Anthony in New York State and in the national women's suffrage movement gave the rural upstate region a particular advantage. Although born in North Adams, Massachusetts, Susan's girlhood years were spent in Battenville (in the eastern section of Greenwich), where her father ran a cotton mill and encouraged his daughters to pursue their educations. Susan, influenced by her Quaker upbringing, became a teacher and taught for a time in Easton (as did her sister Mary), as well as in Greenwich and Fort Edward. Her initial reform work in temperance activity, along with her outrage at the unequal status of women in society, propelled her to the forefront of the women's rights movement. With her lifelong friend and associate, Elizabeth Cady Stanton, Susan energized the suffrage movement throughout the latter half of the 19th century and until her death in 1906. [16]

Susan B. Anthony was a frequent visitor to upstate New York even after she gained national prominence. She was in Lake George at the Fort William Henry Motel in 1856, where she dined while on a break from a speaking tour. She visited the Easton PEC in 1871 and 1875 and wrote the members a letter thanking them for their generous financial support. [17]

She visited friends on Sanford's Ridge in Queensbury, in Warren County, twice in the 1890's. In *Backward Glances II*, author Howard Mason (1964) recounted a story from his friend John Burke about his memory of her visits:

"When I was a child in the early 1890's, Susan B. Anthony visited my parents at the farm home on Sanford's Ridge on two different occasions, and the impression I got was that she was doing something that wasn't just right; at least, when her name was mentioned among my elders, there would be queer expressions or raised eyebrows."[18]

In 1894, at the age of seventy-four, Susan embarked upon a county-by-county tour of New York, ending with a speaking engagement in Glens Falls on April 28. [19]

By the turn of the 20th century, suffrage activity in the Warren, Washington, and Saratoga counties area was indeed growing. The more active organizations of rural Washington County were augmented by quieter, although staunch, support in Warren County. An informal suffrage club had been formed in Glens Falls by 1914. Public forums about suffrage were held in Lake George during the same time period, and momentum was leading up to a statewide vote on the female franchise.[20]

Time and time again, in personal interviews conducted by this author in early years of researching this topic in Glens Falls, local women who remembered suffrage activity expressed a variety of typical orientations: some were away at college during the 1910's and were being exposed to women's rights on their campuses, others were of the opinion that it was considered highly unladylike to clamor for the vote, while others felt that suffrage was quietly supported by most women in Warren County. [21]

While Warren County women were attending lectures for and against suffrage at the Glens Falls Lyceum or attending suffrage teas, Washington County women were attending suffrage schools in Hudson Falls and Fort Edward, under the direction of Elizabeth

Wakeman Mitchell and Laura Schafer Porter, respectively, and participating in the many political equality clubs that had grown up there in the period from 1890 to 1910. [22]

Women were also *reading* about suffrage. *Godey's Lady's Book*, which was the foremost women's magazine of the late 19th century in the United States, contributed to the push for the enhancement of the status of women. However, its founder, Sarah Josepha Hale, who had ties to Warren County (her daughter married the son of Dr. Austin W. Holden, who wrote the 1874 history of Queensbury), considered herself more of a proponent of education for women than a suffragette.[23] Journals published by the American Woman Suffrage Association and the National Woman Suffrage Association, and *The Woman's Journal*, published by the conjoined NAWSA, all helped to educate and motivate women toward the benefits of having the vote.

Newspaper coverage of the issue of suffrage was initially scant in Warren County but became more significant in the months leading up to the statewide vote in November 1917. *The Morning Star, The Republican, The Glens Falls Times and Messenger*, and *The Post Star* carried stories for their Warren County readers. Washington County news coverage was much more prolific – perhaps matching the higher level of suffrage activity there – with *The Washington County Post, The People's Journal, The Greenwich Journal*, and *The Hudson Falls Herald* offering ample articles about the debate. *The Daily Saratogian* covered suffrage news of Saratoga County. [24]

In Warren County, Glens Falls suffrage activities were described to the author in a 1980 letter from Mrs. Carter Hall, the former Hilda Tait, whose father George Tait was the owner of Tait Paper and Color Industries, Inc. (later the Imperial Paper and Color Company). She wrote: "We really slipped so quietly into women's suffrage that there was hardly a ripple. I was introduced to women's suffrage when I was at Vassar [College] and just accepted it and then went back to Glens Falls....[....]...I don't think there was any real issue or that it was a burning question in Glens Falls other than to get the vote. We just slid into it, and there was no violent reaction. I think it was because the electorate was so intelligent." [25]

A weekly column, "Noted Men Tell Why They Are For Suffrage," appeared in *The Glens Falls Times and Messenger* throughout 1917. Hilda Tait's father, George Tait, wrote for the October 30 issue, making reference to the Midwestern states that had recently granted women the vote:

"To the Suffragists:
Yes, you are surely coming like a great energetic Western breeze. You stepped over Iowa from Kansas and captured Illinois with scarce the skirmish of a battle; then you stride over another gap and are likewise taking the great middle state of Ohio and now the mighty Empire State evidently hangs in the balance.   You appear never to be vanquished, a negative decision of  the polls produces renewed activity.  When you win this New York State may your highest ideals be in evidence.   You will find fads and follies of your own sex, especially in the larger centers of activities, needing your greatest reforming care so that when you judge the brethren of full-fledged citizenship may the purest and best of womanhood dominate and influence not merely the legislative but much more the civic life.
Yours in such hope,
GEORGE TAIT" [26]

The Men's League for Suffrage in Warren County scheduled speaking visits to every town in the county that year as part of their campaign on behalf of women. This group included:  Dr. Charles O. Judkins, Dr. Caughey, Daniel F. O'Keefe, Professor Sears, and Elmer West. [27]

In the days before the November 6 vote, state, regional, and local suffrage activity intensified.  A statewide suffrage parade and rally was held in New York City, and regional newspapers described it in vivid and colorful detail.  Marchers there who represented Warren County were:  Mrs. C.J. Nordstrom, Mrs. Carter (Hilda Tait) Hall, Milla Fish, Myrtle Merrill, Mrs. A. M. Wilkie, Mrs. Martin L.C. Wilmarth, Clara Griffin, Mrs. Elmer J. West, Mrs. D.E. VanWirt, and Kersten Taube.  A small men's division took part in the parade also representing the county were Carter Hall (Hilda Tait's husband) and George Foster Peabody. [28]

George Foster Peabody, of Saratoga Springs and Lake George, who was a nationally known financier and philanthropist, was affiliated with the Spencer Trask investment firm.  In the late 1800's, he gave Prospect Mountain and Hearthstone Park (in Warren County) to the State of New York.  He was a man interested in many worthy funds and causes and had the distinction of being the President of the Men's League for Woman Suffrage in New York State.  He went on to serve as one of Franklin Delano Roosevelt's "Brain Trusters." Peabody's wife in his later years was the lovely and regal Katrina Trask, widow of his best friend and business partner, Spencer Trask, and one who shared his passion for the arts and culture, as well as for social and political causes like suffrage and international peace.  Katrina Trask (who will be discussed further in Chapter 8) championed the rights of women, designating Lake George lakeside retreat, Wiawaka, as a vacation spot for the factory girls of the Troy, New York garment mills. [29]

Peabody's and Trask's summer neighbor on "Millionaire's Row" in Bolton Landing on Lake George, Dr. Mary Putnam Jacobi, was also a strong advocate for women's suffrage (and will be discussed further in Chapter 7).   Mary Jacobi was the first woman to attend the foremost medical school, L'École de Médicine, in Paris.   She addressed the Constitutional Convention in Albany in 1894 on the topic of female enfranchisement and authored the well-known pamphlet, *Common Sense Applied to Woman Suffrage*. [30]

Another summertime Bolton Landing resident, Mary Hillard Loines, of Brooklyn, was an ardent suffragist, as well as an anti-slavery activist.  She was honored at the 1919 NAWSA convention as being the only delegate who had attended the first American Equal Rights (AERA) Convention in 1869.

A listing of the leading figures of the women's rights movement with connections to northern New York would not be complete without a tribute to Inez Milholland, of Lewis, in Essex County.  As the epitome of the 20th century's New Woman – educated, free-thinking, career-minded, cultured – Inez rose to prominence in the national suffrage movement. She gained notoriety as the glamorous woman in white atop the white horse riding at the helm of suffrage parades in New York City and Washington D.C. in the early 1910's. She was a charismatic spokeswoman who articulated the feminist agenda of voting rights and social reform to a new generation of suffragists who were mourning the loss of their longtime leaders, Stanton and Anthony, by the early 1900's. When, at age thirty, Inez collapsed in exhaustion during a speech in which she was exhorting President Woodrow Wilson to support the federal suffrage amendment – and then died a month later – she became the martyr of the suffrage movement. Her contribution was lauded by the National Woman's Party (NWP) at the time of the ratification of the Nineteenth Amendment in August 1920. [31]

Inez's "Forward Into Light" mantra was also heralded in an amazing celebration held at the Milholland estate, Meadowmount, in Lewis, New York in 1924. Perfectly orchestrated by NWP leader Alice Paul, it was meant to coincide with the 1924 elections, the first nationwide contests in which women candidates could run for office. One thousand women from the Essex County and Adirondack region participated in this spectacular pageant. 10,000 people journeyed from around the country – crowding the narrow routes to rural Lewis -- to attend. This event was the last and largest gathering of feminists in the United States until the 1960's. [32]

Newspapers in Warren, Washington, and Saratoga counties on November 7, 1917 were jubilant with the news of the state suffrage victory. Statewide, suffrage passed by 80,000 votes. In Warren County, however, it was dealt a blow – being defeated by only nineteen votes. The city of Glens Falls supported suffrage by 179 votes. It was soundly supported by Washington County and Saratoga County voters as well. [33]

Women in these counties went to the polls to exercise their right to vote in the elections of 1918. An editorial in *The Hudson Falls Herald* from November 7 of that year sums up nicely the significance of those contests:

"Women in this state last Tuesday exercised for the first time the voting privilege in equality with men.  They responded to the new call in good spirit – thoughtfully and seriously.  If the 'Home' suffered – the signs of suffering have not yet appeared.  If woman lost anything of her womanly graces – the loss has yet to be observed.  Quite the contrary – we believe the great day of citizenship became enriched by their participation.  They made November 5, 1918 a day in history, for on that day the last step toward democracy in this state was taken." [34]

Nationwide, the women's suffrage movement struggled as the 19th century neared the 20th.  Aging leaders Susan B. Anthony and Elizabeth Cady Stanton slowed down their travel and lecturing schedules as age, health, and family obligations intervened.  Personalities and agendas on the national level intersected and hit roadblocks, even among loyal suffragists who had worked together for decades.  The frustrations over the elusive suffrage prize began to take their toll as the tactics used were ratcheted up in an effort to claim victory in the fight for the vote.  Stanton's publication of *The Woman's Bible* in 1895 led a large segment of the women's rights movement to veer away from her, as her bible was considered by some to be too self-righteous and feminist -- and a sacrilege to the real Bible.

A younger generation of suffragists came on the scene – some of whom had been trained in the radical and militant techniques of British suffragettes, like Emmeline Pankhurst.  One such person was idealistic Quaker lawyer, Alice Paul, who joined with her best friend, Lucy Burns, to expand the base of women's suffrage support to young, urban, working class, and immigrant women.

At first considered to be too radical for the more conservative, mainstream, branch of NAWSA, Alice Paul and her Congressional Union (CU) – later called the National Woman's Party  (NWP) -- earned legitimacy.  Having learned the efficacy of incorporating the strategies of civil disobedience, hunger strikes, the use of publicity, and the rights of assembly into the suffrage fight, Alice Paul led the NWP to effectively lobby presidential candidates in the 1916 election. A skilled political thinker and strategist, Paul was also an originator of the idea of interjecting the notion of *beauty* and the *modern woman of the 20th century* into the campaign to win passage of a federal suffrage amendment. New ideals of femininity and women political figures were put front and center as leaders of suffrage parades in northeastern cities like New York City and Washington D.C. were striking beauties – like Inez Milholland of rural Essex County, New York, the new symbol of intelligent femininity and a New Woman for the 20th century.

The brilliance of forming a coalition between Alice Paul's National Woman's Party and Carrie Chapman Catt's National American Woman Suffrage Association was demonstrated, however, in a most tragic incident. Known as "The Night of Terror" and taking place on November 15, 1917 (only nine days after New York granted women the right to vote), dozens of suffragists -- working class, middle class, wealthy, and immigrant, of all ages – were jailed by federal police in Washington D.C. after being arrested for peacefully picketing President Woodrow Wilson in front of the White House. The outrage of Americans at the sight of women being roughed up and treated violently by male policemen as they were hauled away for incarceration in abhorrent conditions at the Occoquan Prison workhouse was too much too bear. Leaders of the picketing, including Alice Paul herself, were subjected to barbaric methods of force-feeding when the jailed suffragists went on a hunger strike in protest of their imprisonment. This horrifying event in the history of women's suffrage was depicted in an excellent 2004 Home Box Office (HBO®) movie, *Iron-Jawed Angels*.[35]

The irony of the United States government violently oppressing its female citizens who were lawfully protesting in support of their right to vote – a mainstay of American democracy – while American soldiers were fighting for democracy on European soil in World War I was a powerful catalyst for change. In fact, this incident caused a change in stance on the part of President Wilson, who had not originally been in support of a federal suffrage amendment. The "Winning Strategy" crafted by Carrie Chapman Catt, and aided by building consensus with the NWP and eradicating barriers across socioeconomic, racial, and ethnic categories worked, and, in 1920 a century of struggle for women bore an exhausted victory.

New attitudes about the roles of women – legal, political, social, and economic – resulted, and new definitions of womanhood for the 20th century replaced the narrowly defined attitudes of femininity of the Victorian era. The strengths of the "weaker sex" had been revealed, the power of womanly influence had been demonstrated, and the importance of coalitions of grassroots urban and rural suffrage organizations had been proven. Despite division, debate, and drama, the women's suffrage movement had succeeded in achieving its goal on a national level and had facilitated the development of a new political consciousness for American women that would position them effectively for the challenges of being citizens in 20th century society.

In Easton, New York, as well as across America, a new day for women had dawned.

# Chapter III

## The Effect of Rural Life
## on Female Political Identity in the Modern Era

Easton, New York in 1891 was poised on the precipice of participation in one of the most dramatic and cataclysmic political rights movements in United States history.

The ability to examine the origins of political, civil, or social change in 19th century America requires an understanding of the interplay between individual action and the influences of rural and urban life, regionalism, philosophical tenets of democracy, gender, class, and race in an industrializing society. Once again, dichotomies exist: where there is *cause and effect* to be found among the religious and moral fervor of Quaker abolitionists, for example, there is also the conundrum of women at odds with other women over the question of equal rights and suffrage. The contradictions at work in social reform in the 1800's created a complexity which at times impeded progress for so-called *just causes* (like temperance, education for women, abolition, and equal rights). And, yet, the gyrations of change and dissent added momentum to the reformist movements of this era in American history and remind us of the intricate conditions which, in fact, must be at work and in harmony, in order for true progress to occur.

America in the 19th century was an emerging nation of farms and growing cities. A largely agrarian economy, aided by small mills and industries from the Revolutionary War period, was transforming as mechanization and the Industrial Revolution demanded modifications in rural and urban areas. While rural life remained a solid and traditional way of life for millions, the growth of cities brought new notions of what American society could be. The original 17th century settlement of the northeastern United States was followed by the dominance of the South's cotton economy and

Westward expansion. Waves of European immigrants found their way to American shores in search of a better life – helping to mobilize needed labor for factories and farms, but also adding to the already delicate mix of gender, class, racial, and ethnic forces which were ingredients to the recipe for American progress – and divisions -- in the modern era.

As with any social or political change, the experience of individuals is impacted either marginally or powerfully by their levels of identification and belonging in society. The cocoon of the family blends into the world of friends, of school, of work, and religious and/or philosophical affiliation. Geography is paramount as well, for where a person grows up or lives provides an important cultural *frame of reference* for understanding the world and interacting with others. The experience of an individual within a certain family, or in a specific school, or within a certain state or nation creates a body of ideas and beliefs that become the elements of that person's blueprint for meaning and action in life. Likewise, as it relates to the thesis of this book, these factors contribute to a slate which defines a person's *political identity* within his/her culture or society, rural or urban. Similarly, the attachment of a person to his surroundings and those people (family, friends, neighbors) who inhabit these surroundings, along with its institutions, customs, and traditions, are harbingers of character, philosophical and/or religious belief, physical experience, and human relationships. On a small or grand scale, the individual in a family unit or in a governmental unit (town, state, nation) develops political identity through some or all of these factors and conditions:

> Gender/Biology
> Class/ Socioeconomic status/ Wealth
> Race
> Ethnicity
> Geography
> Philosophical influences
> Education
> Religion
> Intellectual influences
> Interpersonal exposures
> Family

Cross-cultural influences
Language/Cognitive Framework
Psychology
Time period/ Historical framework
Political climate/Political parties
Local/State/ National/ Global perspective
Personal experiences
Mentors
Morality

The intersection and interplay of these various elements predispose an individual to attachment to certain people, groups, ideologies, and causes.  However, *gender* identity is certainly overriding – as put forth in this book, which is about a gender issue, and how it played out in a rural upstate New York town on the cusp of the modern era.

Stepping back for a moment to look at femininity and its various definitions over the ages, it is clear that women have had many adjectives with which to contend – either to model themselves after, or to rebel against – depending on their desires to conform with society's prevailing notion of what is *womanly* at a particular time in history, or to march to their own drummers and be versions of *feminine* that are based on individual self-worth and unique attributes.  While the scope of this book will not trace the definitions of femininity in any comprehensive way, the tenet that what was considered feminine *did* transform over time and in various environments creating both problems and opportunities for women in America is supported here.  The *cult of domesticity* arising from the post-Revolutionary War era confined women to a life centered on the home, farm, and family where marriage and motherhood were paramount to female identity and purpose.  The Victorian period continued this societal view of women, in both rural and urban areas, as the purveyors of the domestic arts, keepers of hearth and home, gentle, acquiescing, and subservient, and not suited to the public sphere inhabited by men. Women were to be prized for their beauty, grace, and softness, and for character traits that involved nurturing and supporting the men in their lives. They were not to venture into what was considered *unladylike* -- like politics, education, or business.

While such was the broad generalization of what constituted the female realm, many examples existed of women operating out of the domestic sphere for a myriad of reasons, not the least of which were the customs and mores of regions where economic conditions led women to break through traditional barriers to societal and civic participation.

By the 1890's, definitions of femininity were changing across America, and the accepted view of women as passive, dependent, and servile was being called into question.   Conventional ways of thinking about women in society, in marriage, and in the family were facing harsh examination by increasingly large numbers of women who were joining together to fight for greater rights for their gender. [1] Women's history expert Kaye Stearman traced the use of the term "new woman" in contemporary periodicals and books to about 1894 and estimated 1895 as the date when the term "feminist" started appearing in print to describe the women and men who were organizing in support of equal rights and more equitable treatment for women. [2]

One of the most famous books ever written about the female gender and feminism was Simone de Beauvoir's *The Second Sex*, published in France in 1908.  Delving into the psychology of femininity, how society reacts to gender differences, and the implication for women that these create, de Beauvoir exposed the origins of *the weaker sex* theory that became part of the conventional view of what constituted the proper roles of women.  Writing just after the turn of the 20th century, she declared that society had come to deem that "humanity is male, and male defines woman not in herself, but as relative to him; she is not regarded as an autonomous being." [3]   She exposed the prevailing view that "to be feminine is to be weak, futile, docile." [4] Putting forth the idea that feminine qualities – such as coquetry, appearance, housekeeping – become, in themselves, a woman's vocation in life, what society considered a "true woman" was nothing more than an artificial creation of civilization. [5]

When such attitudes and theories about women in the 19th and early 20th centuries are given the overlay of urban and rural environments, the variation in what was feminine and womanly can be seen. As such, common denominators such as geography, family, and economic partnership between men and women become important determinants of how the terms were defined in a given location at a given time. While the urban centers of America created a certain set of conditions which defined roles for women, so the way of life in rural America led to a slate of duties and expectations that both defined the essence of their gender in that environment – and the rhythm of their daily lives.

Noted historian Lois W. Banner described well the experience of rural women in America around the turn of the 20th century and offered support for the idea (supported by the thesis of this book as well) that there was greater partnership between men and women in rural – versus urban – society which led to more equality for women. In outlining the vast responsibilities of rural women in New England in 1910, Banner described what could well be a typical day in the lives of the ladies of the Easton Political Equality Club in northeastern New York:    "….women [….] bore heavy responsibilities in terms of maintaining the farm, which was typically a family enterprise.  In addition to housekeeping chores, the farm wife cared for the family's vegetable plot and for its supply of livestock for family use.  During harvest time, she cooked around the clock for her family and the farm hands.  Among the majority of farm families who were not wealthy, daughters typically worked as teachers or as domestic servants in other households to supplement the family income.  [….] On the surface, the life of rural women appears busy and uneventful.  Enmeshed in the traditional attitudes of rural culture, herself a mainstay of a conservative Protestant ministry, and geographically isolated from urban sophistication, her adjustment to her role seems foreordained." [6]

How the founding members of the Easton Political Equality Club in 1891 mobilized themselves to join the fight for female political equality is a story about femininity, family, friendship, and the domestic sphere in rural America at the turn of the 20th century. The ability of Lucy Allen, Chloe Sisson, some of their relatives, and many neighbors to tap into their womanliness, be in touch with the rudiments of their identities as civic beings, and conjoin those with a well-developed intellectual understanding of progressive ideologies about women's rights was made possible by blending their reality as rural women with their desire for change. The creation of the PEC and the staging area from which it planned and executed its activities for the cause of suffrage was done from the comfort and familiarity of the homes, churches, and institutions of their small, beloved community.

As will be discussed further in the next chapter, the ladies of Easton, from their rural domestic sphere, launched their political fight, traveling on foot and by carriage or wagon, often with their children in tow, in all seasons of the year to keep to a monthly schedule of congregating for education, socialization, religious devotion, and political action. These ladies were not an 1890's version of the 1960's feminist bra burners. To be sure, their cause of equal suffrage was still a brazen idea -- even at that late decade of the 19th century – but there is no indication that the larger community of Easton gave the PEC members a bad time over their ideas. There is no evidence to suggest that they were maligned or widely criticized, or even that their husbands and male relatives were opposed to their participation in this cause.

Lucy, Chloe, and their friends assembled peacefully and productively, with the apparent support of family and community, and exhibited an acute sense of civic duty and political acumen in organizing to promote suffrage. They formed friendships and alliances and educated each other in monthly meetings about literary, historical, and governmental issues, and wrote letters to their state representatives in Albany, New York's state capital. They were inspired by national suffrage leaders and mentored through their letters and lectures, and in spirit. Like astute activists, they sought to extend their reach, assisting neighboring rural communities like

Cambridge and Shushan to form PECs, and across the county line to Valley Falls in Rensselear County. They partnered with the local chapter of the WCTU, showing their understanding of the advantageous relationship of liquor reform with women's rights. Even as white rural women, they spoke out in favor of the plight of the urban female factory workers of the Troy, New York textile mills, many of whom were young, poor, and of various ethnic backgrounds.

The incredible work of the Easton PEC was carried out amid the formidable chores and responsibilities of the members' farms and families. They did not strike out in revolt against their husbands or fathers – handing them stove pots as they marched out the door for a political meeting. Quite the contrary, chores were completed, meals were made, children were cared for, mending was done, animals were tended to, and husbands' needs were met – all while the political work of fighting for the franchise was carried on.

This fact, in part, accounts for the importance of looking at rural geography and regionalism as adding variety to the methods for winning suffrage across 19th century America. It was the western territories and states, starting with Wyoming in 1869, that gave credence to the idea that the rugged conditions in the new, rural areas being settled across America, along with a pioneering spirit and democratic ideals that typically accompany that kind of settlement, could lead to more equality between the sexes. This way of life tended to predispose the West, and rural areas, to grant full citizenship rights, including voting, to women. The partnership of men and women, husbands and wives, in situations of working the land, raising a family, battling the forces of nature, and earning a living is of prime importance, and the contribution of each partner was essential. Such conditions tended to breed an egalitarian attitude between the sexes. Such was the case in Easton, too.

Division of labor by gender has biological and anthropological origins, so to argue that one gender has a more valued role in society is without foundation (in the view of this author). The character of relations between men and women, for the reasons noted above, as the West was settled is today commonly accepted by suffrage historians as an explanation for the greater acceptance of female political equality in that region, and, therefore, earlier enfranchisement.

It is reasonable to extrapolate this same sense of gender respect, interdependence, and cooperation to the rural areas of the northeast United States, and specifically to the rural areas of upstate New York, where there is a strong tradition of valuing family roots and where the fortitude of the male-female bond is a determinant of success in the agricultural economy.

While the urban centers of the Northeast were carrying on their own strategies for winning the vote for women, rural communities adapted methods, rhetoric, and action to complement their unique circumstances and way of life. The magnificence of this variation is what is seen in the style of suffrage work of the Easton PEC, as well as in the activities of the women in neighboring villages like Hudson Falls and Fort Edward. Likewise, the brand of suffrage work done by women of the nearby cities of Glens Falls and Saratoga Springs reflected their particular lifestyles and socioeconomic class, and their meeting places were the buildings and institutions of the downtown districts. Similarities and differences, contradictions and complexities, abound when comparing and contrasting the methods used by the women of the rural and urban areas of upstate New York.

The fascination perhaps is to examine to what extent the self-definition of these women included the notion of using the elements of their *virtuous womanhood* to achieve their goal. Surely, the brilliance of rural women in Easton in particular in employing their gender identities within the domestic sphere for political expediency aided them in reaching this goal. Add to this a sharp understanding of their rights of assembly, speech, and petitioning the government, and it is easy to see that, while they and the other suffragists of the rural areas of Washington, Warren, and Saratoga counties may have been political novices, they quickly rose to the challenge of demanding equal treatment as citizens under a democratic government.

Reformist sentiment was strong in these three upstate New York counties in the 19th century, and the influence of national leaders was felt decisively there.  For the cause of temperance, noted men like Judge Reuben Walworth of Saratoga Springs, and E.C. Delevan of Ballston Spa were orators of great notoriety.  On the issue of anti-slavery, abolitionists Frederick Douglass, Gerrit Smith, and William Lloyd Garrison traveled this region, often joining forces with temperance and women's suffrage advocates.  Joining forces also sometimes included marriage – as when abolitionist activist Angelina Grimké of Massachusetts wed Reverend Theodore Weld, an abolitionist leader originally from Granville, in northern Washington County.  In addition, Elizabeth Cady Stanton's husband, Henry, was a leader in the American and New York anti-slavery societies, along with Weld, Smith, and Garrison, and Elizabeth herself was a strong supporter of this work.

Susan B. Anthony, who began her political activist career as a temperance leader and ardent supporter of abolition, understood the strong interplay of alliances and sought the opportunity to encourage women of the upstate region to address their lack of political equality and to begin to develop civic leadership skills through participation in reformist organizations.

A chapter of the Women's Christian Temperance Union was formed in Easton in 1888 and flourished until 1920. Like the PEC, meetings were held at the Methodist Church or at Marshall Seminary (no longer extant).  Although only a handful of women were at the organizational meeting, membership grew after 1892 (the year after the establishment of the PEC), and numbered seventy members by 1920, then declined between 1920 and its demise in 1945. Fundraising was a continuous problem, and minutes of the Easton PEC show that its members gave periodic donations of money to the WCTU for the temperance cause.  Once again, the support between the two organizations – moral and financial – demonstrated that the members of both groups were attentive to a breadth of women's rights issues and were cooperating together on them. [7]

The significance of mentoring and inspiration of national reform movement leaders, like Susan B. Anthony, can also be seen in the influence of Frances E. Willard, renowned president of the national WCTU from 1881 to 1898, in the creation of the Easton chapter -- and also in the creation of the Easton PEC. The Easton PEC Yearbook (in the collection of the Easton Library) from the years 1910 – 1911 contains this quote: "If prayer and womanly influence are doing so much for God by indirect methods, how shall it be when the elective force is brought to bear through the battery of the ballot box. – Frances E. Willard." Clearly, the brand of womanly influence at the very core of the mission of the PEC found a spiritual guidepost in the writings of this feminist reform leader. The sensibility of the Easton women to national reform issues that were being debated in the late 1890's well beyond the agrarian landscape of their small town reveals them as sophisticated and forward-thinking reformers in their own right.

The primacy of the agricultural environment of Easton was a determinant in the unique styling of the PEC as well as in the missions of the other local organizations that existed there in the late 1800's. While it cannot be known what levels of education the adult men and women of Easton had achieved, what is clear is that they hungered for knowledge and sought forums for debate and discussion about improvements in agriculture and in educating their young people in the farming tradition.

The Easton Lyceum, formed as a debating society in the late 1870's, met in the South Friends (Quaker) Meeting House and later moved to Marshall Seminary, which was nearby, on today's Route 40. The Lyceum eventually broadened its focus to literary and cultural programs and served to provide intellectual stimulus and opportunities for communal gathering for a town whose economy was focused on manual labor. Active in the Lyceum were PEC leader Lucy Allen and her husband, George.[8]

The Easton Farmers' Club was founded in 1876 by a "group of nine farmers above average in intelligence and education." [9]   The lofty purpose of the club was described by member F.O. Ives: "It is well to improve our methods of farming and also the fertility of our soil, but it is of far greater importance that we should improve ourselves and our condition.  The object of our meeting is to develop a better and higher mankind and womankind among ourselves, to enhance the comforts and attractiveness of our homes and to strengthen our attachments to our pursuits."[10] Like the Lyceum, the PEC, and the WCTU, the Farmers' Club counted men and women among its members, and young people were included in auxiliary activities. Member and secretary (and eventual PEC member) Lydia Hoag wrote in her March 10, 1883 minutes:  "Agriculture is no mean calling. It is a science of a high order......Farmers are beginning to understand more perfectly what improved agriculture implies.  It means improved farm machinery; it means improved breeds of farm stock. It means more than all these.  It means that our farms be brought into that degree of productiveness which shall yield the best possible results.  Agriculture is the lever which moves all the other industries of the world.  When farmers fully comprehend this, then, and not till then, will the mission of the Farmers' Club be ended." [11]

The Easton Grange was formed in 1907 [12] – largely due to the impetus from the PEC, as its minutes' book from that year documents. [13]

The notion that farming was not only an occupation or livelihood but also a scientific pursuit that required their utmost intellectual involvement was a mindset that prevailed in Easton during the years of the late 19th century. This mindset carried over to several of the other local organizations, as mentioned above, whose memberships and participation revealed gender equality.  Ancillary to this, the strong bonds of friendship formed by the members – who were relatives and neighbors – of all of these clubs strengthened the cooperation and effectiveness of them. This rural tradition of male-female equality, in combination with a matrix of local clubs and institutions which fostered it, surely influenced the reasons behind the founding of the PEC in 1891, as well as its chosen methods of promotion of the suffrage cause.

Easton PEC leaders Lucy Allen and Chloe Sisson capitalized on a genuine mutual affection and a shared commitment to a cause -- both of which would propel their local PEC into high gear and become a model for the creation of more PECs in the region. Never once did they, or the ladies of the Easton PEC, forget or negate their femininity, their roles as farm wives, mothers, and church members. Instead, they utilized their womanly influence to create an organization devoted to enhancing political equality for the female gender. They were not shunned for their ideas or activities, but instead turned the once-unheard-of notion of female suffrage into an accepted idea based on the legitimacy of their message as women citizens. Through their participation and leadership in the rural organizations of Easton, the members of the PEC sharpened their political skills and showed their reform-minded orientation. As such, they were able to create a political organization with power and influence, and based on their political identities as rural women within the domestic sphere.

# Chapter IV
## The Easton Political Equality Club:
## Embracing Femininity for a Noble Cause

On December 17, 1891, a notice appeared in *The People's Journal* in Greenwich, New York, announcing a meeting for those interested in joining the Political Equality Club (PEC) in neighboring Easton. And, thus, the national fight for women's suffrage, which had started in rural Seneca Falls, New York forty-three years earlier, finally made its way to this rural area in the northeastern part of the state.

A clue to the very distinct brand of suffrage sentiment that would define the Easton PEC can be found in the words of this December 17 newspaper article: "Let no man or woman be mistaken as to what this movement for woman's suffrage really means. We, none of us, wish to turn the world upside down, or to convert women into men. We desire women, on the contrary, above all things to continue womanly in the highest and best sense – and to bring their true women's influence, on behalf of whatsoever things are true, honest, just, pure, lovely, and of good report, to bear upon the conduct of public affairs. Lend a hand." [1]

What would happen in Easton over the next twenty-five plus years as state and federal enfranchisement were sought after revealed a fundamental definition of womanliness and femininity – *"true, honest, just, pure, lovely, and of good report"* – that uplifted and guided the members of the PEC to their goal. From the very start of their organization, they demonstrated that they would not compromise their womanliness – but instead would use the strength of it to promote their cause. In so doing, they showed themselves to be women with heightened gender- and self- awareness who were sensitive to the transformation in women's roles in society and in the home as the 20th century was about to dawn.

Without a doubt, the ladies of Easton were familiar with the language and rhetoric of the national women's suffrage movement and may have noticed that their bold statements on behalf of femininity put them at odds with the more typical strategies which tied suffrage to a quest to overcome oppression by men.   In fact, their outright declarations of their womanliness – and their wish *not* to turn themselves into men through their suffrage work -- may have seemed more akin to the message of *anti*-suffragists, who openly used the mores and customs of the Victorian era and what defined the ideal Victorian lady to assert that women had no place in the political sphere.  So, for the women of Easton to not only put their femininity on display for a political cause and to declare that they would use this womanliness as a weapon to win their fight was, indeed, a fascinating and unique civic tool.  Their own consciousness as women allowed them to challenge commonly held ideas of how women should behave in society and to assert their constitutional rights in devising an operational stance for suffrage which would mesh effectively with their lives as rural farm women.

These were confident women – confident of their roles in their homes and in the community, knowing that they were indispensable to the farm economy that was their families' livelihood.  They were pious women – women of Protestant and Quaker faiths – whose overall spiritual sense guided them, more so than any particular religious affiliation.  These were women with strong family ties and with a sense of neighborliness and intense bonds of friendship.

Once again, the grounding of relationships in the rural town of Easton was, in part, based on the depth of connections that occur between people who share the same environment --  who help each other during times of need, farm on neighboring farms, assist each other at births and deaths and marriages and sicknesses, worship together, endure hardships as they battle weather and the greater forces of nature --  in order to make a living as farmers and to raise their families.  Certainly, there is a camaraderie in this way of life; and, certainly, among the women, who are keepers of hearth and home, the importance of a network of family and friends was vital to their well-being, if not their very survival.   In this context, the women of small town Easton, even with its several hamlets – Barker's Grove, North Easton, Bang All, Beadle Hill, Briggs Corner, Easton Corners, and Crandall's Corners – were a tight-knit group.  And, never let it be said that they were *just* rural farm women; they were truly multi-dimensional people with high intelligence, acute political sensibilities, and a true understanding of the profound civil rights movement of which they were a part, as their writings verify.

The origins and work of the Easton PEC were eloquently summarized in the beautifully-written history by founding member, Chloe Sisson, which was presented in Chapter One.  The fortitude of the founding (as well as subsequent) members over three decades is evident in this piece, as is the use of traditional female characteristics in their suffrage activities.  Sewing, for example – for the creation of suffrage banners and for the making of the exquisite rag dolls to raise money at the National Suffrage Bazaar – was a highly regarded skill on the part of the members.  In addition, womanliness and femininity for the ladies of the PEC at the turn of the 20th century also encompassed such qualities and talents as: a mastery of the domestic arts, a competency in farming and animal husbandry, mothering and caring for families, piety and religious involvement, morality and benevolence, and intellectual enrichment.    Truly, through an examination of the minutes of PEC meetings, these elements of their female make-up shine through and reveal a very complex and sophisticated political consciousness on the part of the members.

In the words of Lucy Allen, the president of the Easton PEC during its most active years and also the president of the Washington County branch of the New York State Woman Suffrage Party,  suffrage was the critical mission: "We stand together in firm faith that knows no weakening, that the elevating of women means the elevating of humanity, and that no nobler cause can engage the time and thoughts of intelligent beings." [2]  Mrs. Allen, a respected leader as well as a gracious and feminine presence in suffrage work in northeastern New York, was a gifted orator.  She articulated brilliantly the special blend of strength and womanliness that would characterize the Easton PEC throughout its years of service to its *noble cause*.

In handwritten notes in her personal composition book, Lucy Allen wrote her remarks for a debate on "The Industrial [Economic] Side of Woman Suffrage," which took place at Burton Hall on February 25, 1910. (Burton Hall was built in 1901 and replaced the Marshall Seminary as a public gathering place; today, it is the Town Hall.) Included in these remarks is the following quote in which she describes the ladies of the PEC:

"The majority of us are farmers' wives here in Easton and our husbands are perfect – we are so well-housed, so soft-bedded, and so loving cared for that our tendency is to forget that Easton isn't the whole world, that there are other women not as we are. Yet industrial [economic] conditions are open to some slight criticism even in this paradise of Easton. First of all, we want to get rid of this fallacy that marriage is a state of being supported. Since our men are mainly the gatherers of money – we mistakenly assume that they are the creators of wealth. They are not. The man gives his daily labor toward earning board and clothes, but what he receives cannot be eaten or worn. It is nothing till he puts it into his wife's hands and her intelligence, energy, and ability transforms the raw material. Until this is done no man can receive anything worth having. He begins and she completes the making of their joint wealth. The man turns his labor into money, the woman turns the money into usable material. Their dependence is mutual. She supports him exactly as he supports her." 3

Boldly stated by Mrs. Allen in this public debate were the qualities and characteristics that defined the members of the Easton PEC: strength, transcendence of womanly virtue and industriousness, partnership and mutual dependence with their husbands, refusal to be defined as the oppressed gender, recognition of the primacy of their varied roles as women in a rural farm economy – and *equality*.

The PEC meetings themselves, from 1891 until the passage of the federal suffrage amendment in 1920, are the ideal way of examining the inner workings of the club, its methods, its leaders, and its impact on the cause of women's suffrage locally, regionally, and statewide. Sadly, the records in their entirety no longer exist; however, a minutes book which includes the years 1906 through 1910 *does* exist (in the Easton Library) and was relied upon heavily in the writing of this book.  Likewise, articles from local newspapers like *The People's Journal* (which began publication in 1842 in Greenwich and was later renamed *The Greenwich Journal and Salem Press* ) and *The Washington County Post* (called "America's Oldest Weekly Newspaper" and tracing its origin to 1778 in nearby Cambridge) document the lively and active work of the Easton PEC up through the second decade of the 20th century.

As early as 1871, there were rumblings of the women's suffrage issue in Easton.  On January 27, 1871, *The Washington County Post* reported this story with an Easton byline: "On 16th instant, Susan B. Anthony electrified an audience at the [Friends] Seminary [in the hamlet of Barker's Grove in South Easton] by stating that woman is already a voter by the fourteenth and fifteenth amendments to the Constitution, and advising them [the women] to organize at once and not fail to put in an appearance at the next election." [4]

A return trip to Easton for the national suffrage leader in 1875 hinted at the favorable sentiment toward the issue: "Miss Susan B. Anthony gave a lecture at the Seminary last week Sunday evening on her favorite theme.  The lecture was well-attended, and although many new and radical ideas were advanced, was well-received." [5]

While women could not vote in state or national elections, they could, in various places in New York and around the country, vote in school district elections. Why this disparity existed historically one can only conjecture, although there is evidence to suggest it was a haphazard experiment in including women in the electorate for a specific purpose – education – that could be said to come under the umbrella of maternal interests.  In 1880, the New York State legislature granted to women who had children or who paid taxes the right to vote in school district official elections, and also to hold office on school boards.  The following article appeared in *The People's Journal* on October 12, 1882:

" Easton. – A handsome victory won. At the district school meeting at Barker's Grove, in Easton, James B. Allen was chosen chairman. Nineteen women voted. For trustee 55 votes were cast.  On the first formal ballot Miss Julia A. Batty [who would later be an active member of the PEC] received 36; Dr. R. Slocum 18; scattering, 1.  A majority of 17 overall.  Mrs. Eliza Wood was elected secretary, and Mrs. Susie Crandall collector.  The trustee was voted unlimited power to new seat, and [to] make such other needed repairs as she should deem best in the schoolhouse, furnish fuel, etc.  No uncouth language or tobacco smoke polluted the atmosphere.  Talk about Reform! Reform!! Reform !!! This is head and shoulders above the great Tilden Reform!  Three cheers for school district at Barker's Grove in Easton, N.Y." [6]

By the following week, the influence of women through the school vote was being reported: "The district school meeting in town was more spirited than usual, as might have been expected, the women proved good at electioneering in districts, carried off all the honors offices. A trial may prove them more effective than men." [7]  In 1892, New York State ruled that women could vote in county school commissioner elections, or to run for that post.  School suffrage, therefore, gave women some semblance of electoral participation, albeit limited, prior to full suffrage, which was granted in 1917.

The very first public notice of the intent to gather local women (and men, too) of Easton to work to correct the gender inequality of enfranchisement appeared in *The People's Journal* on October 8, 1891: "At the request of the State Woman Suffrage Association, a meeting will be held at the Seminary Saturday afternoon, October 10 at 2:30 to organize a Political Equality Club.  The object of which shall be the enfranchisement of women, and their equality before the law. The masses are at last beginning to recognize its justice on the ground of expediency in dealing with the evils of the day." [8]

The October 29 issue reported on this organizational meeting: "[At the Political Equality Club] there was much genuine interest manifested in this movement, and several names were recorded as members.  In many places as here it is found that the women's suffrage sentiment is ripe, and only needs organization to put in active service, and there is little doubt that Washington County will no longer be behind in this work." [9]

In this same weekly edition, a summary of the remarks of Reverend Mr. Ogden, minister of the Presbyterian Church in Easton, in his weekly sermon hinted at the growing acceptance of political equality for women, as well as the very real influence of womanhood in a reform-minded turn-of-the-century nation.  Rev. Ogden spoke of female enfranchisement, saying: "The whole society has been changed.  The legal status of wives, mothers, and widows has been greatly modified; education, self-support and opportunity have been accorded to women; a larger conception of womanhood prevails and the days of women's subjection are nearly ended......The agitation of the women's suffrage question for half a century has made possible the large work of women day-to-day in education, philanthropy, reform, and co-operative work.  Whatever may be the fate of the plan for a national federation of women, one thing is certain, women have learned the omnipotence and happiness of co-operative work and the weakness and weariness of that which is isolated; and this is sure to make them more fruitful of accomplishment hereafter, whether their plans of work shall include themselves, their homes and their children, society or the nation. For the cause that lacks assistance, 'gainst the wrong that needs resistance, for the future in the distance, there's a woman's right to do!" [10]

Notices continued to appear in *The People's Journal* about the Easton PEC and its activities throughout the fall, inviting people interested in "the advancement of women" [11] to come to its meetings.

Newspaper coverage in *The People's Journal* about the PEC continued, in fact, from the inception of the club in 1891 to well into the 1910's, verifying its legitimacy and its status as a beacon of reform in the rural regions of upstate New York.   Reporting mentioned the array of intellectually stimulating topics which were discussed at the meetings, and papers that were read, such as: " The Principles of the Republican Party, The Principles of the Democratic Party, The Rise of the People's Party and Its Principles, A Brief History of the Prohibition Party, and the Relation of Each of These to Woman Suffrage."[12]

The symbiotic, cooperative bond between the Easton chapter of the Women's Christian Temperance Union (WCTU) and the PEC is also documented in *The People's Journal* throughout the 1890's and early 1900's. The Easton WCTU, which had been formed in December 1888, found a philosophical partner in the PEC and some of their members were also members of the suffrage club. The bridge between the temperance cause and women's suffrage became more firm as women began to see the cause and effect between their ability to have a real voice in liquor reform through the advancement of their right to vote. The power of the ballot was thought to be the tool by which the deleterious effects of liquor and intoxication on men, women, children, the home, and society could be rectified.

It appears that at least one resident of South Easton interpreted the connection between the WCTU and the PEC as a dangerous one. A March 23, 1893 column by the editor of *The People's Journal* mentioned a letter received from a correspondent who was clearly upset over the supposed trouble being caused by both organizations in town. Disagreeing artfully with this resident, the editor penned this articulate opinion: "Undoubtedly most of those who read South Easton's mention of the worthy endeavors of Easton's women understood exactly what the writer said and meant. There is no need of a review of that. Correspondent seems to be a little mixed, for instance, 'giving teas, and generally assuming the part of a man.' Cor. [the Correspondent] is surprised to know that the 'women of Easton do nothing but work for the W.C.T.U and other organizations.' If that were true you might well be surprised. Since, however, the organizations include Easton's very best house keepers and home makers and keepers in their number, we are all spared of that distasteful 'surprise.' Mentioning the Political Equality Club, Cor.

says, 'it has been the cause of innumerable strifes.' There is certainly a very great mistake about that statement, as the writer is sure that there has always been perfect good nature and harmony among them. They would endorse this statement were it worth while simply to satisfy those outside. As to the amount of benefit it has been to the town can be better estimated probably when the work is finished and at any time that would depend upon who should be the Judge. 'Does it become a woman's dignity to ride around and induce voters to attend elections?' That depends upon her own standard of dignity. Does it distract from one's dignity to attend to that which he or she may deem to be a duty? Is it a distraction from any one's 'dignity' to walk or ride, when the purpose is to exclude liquor from their own town, when it will keep the father and son from wasting their earnings, from spoiling the home, from losing what 'dignity' there might be in the entire family? The W.C.T.U. advised the movement throughout the county. The Locals appointed these women as a committee; and if any one thinks they lost dignity by the undertaking, let some one approach or reproach them upon the subject. It surely must be 'womanly,' for no woman attempts it who is not sure that something ought to be done in this field of labor, and that she can do some good by it; she can try at least. Suppose we call a body of ladies *missionaries*, who go into foundling hospitals to take out the infants and find homes for them. Are they any the less womanly for their efforts? The woman does not stoop but brings the work up to her plane. Is the woman less a missionary who tries to save homes and people, than she who tries to find homes for the homeless? These acts are womanly which come from noble intentions. It was 'womanly' action upon the part of Cor.' to remind' these faithful women of 'higher and noble purposes.' They have long since been striving with such objects in view. Like Cor., they find it difficult to accomplish any very great amount of good without either writing or publishing or by going out and attending to affairs themselves. Their houses are well-kept. Their husbands, as a rule, do not suffer from neglect, on the contrary they appreciate that their wives are their equals, and not only their helpmates, but that they are unselfish, self-sacrificing, and good. When it is practical and best, they can go with their wives and assist them in their womanly work. If they find any need to "protest,' you may depend upon them to do as they have against liquor licenses and 'taxation without representation.' One of these neglected' husbands in this county, who is Prof. and principal of a good school, took his young lady pupils to election, told them 'he asked them to know how to vote when the time came!' Those 'who *are* wives and mothers,' who find time to devote to others as well as self, not on the principle of so many homes, 'us four and no more,' will not 'shudder' from *imaginary* wrongs in their neighbors' or friends' houses. Their minds are employed with how they can do their own work, and help others to do theirs, how to make their home a beacon of light of labor, love, and charity, to induce those who are in dread, and in obscure places, to come out and improve. The opinion of one or a few, will not effect the work of this generation of women. If Easton were blotted entirely, she would not be missed, more than the meteor that falls. She is not trying to leave but to keep up. The outside world clasp hands over the space where she had been and would do her work for her, and go on." [13]

With this kind of supportive expression being published and read in Easton and its surrounding towns in Washington County, it is clear that the PEC very much had its finger on a hot topic of the day and had gained much legitimacy in its cause even by 1893, the second full year of its existence. Once again, the theme of womanly influence flowed through the words of the newspaper's editor as he lauded the ladies of Easton for their ability to assert themselves as political citizens while succeeding gloriously as wives and mothers with ladylike virtues in the domestic sphere.

The sisterhood and spirit of cooperation that existed between the PEC and the WCTU was also evident in this *People's Journal* article from May 11, 1898, describing a memorial service for illustrious WCTU national president Frances E. Willard: " The Woman's Christian Temperance Union of Easton gave a memorial service Sunday afternoon, at Marshall Hall [Seminary], to Frances E. Willard. A large audience were present and listened with deep interest to the glowing tributes paid Miss Willard. The room was tastefully decorated with the colors of the union and [the] Equality club. Beautiful plants and flowers were seen in profusion, arranged upon the platform. A general display of the stars and stripes were seen. Miss Willard's picture rested upon an easel with a band of white ribbon draped around it. The program of exercises consisted of papers, recitations, and speeches, all in keeping with the occasion. A quartette composed of Messrs. Hoag, Anthony, and the Misses Shearer and Slocum, gave sweet music. Great credit rests with the ladies of the union in arranging the affair. All who took part are deserving of a share." [14]

While the local Easton PEC and WCTU shared a strong cooperative sentiment for their respective reformist missions of suffrage and temperance, directives from the New York State Woman Suffrage Association (NYSWSA) kept the local political equality clubs on message and involved in state-level suffrage activities -- and also reminded them that the National American Woman Suffrage Association (NAWSA) was not a political party. This point of clarification was placed as an official notice at the conclusion of this article about the NYSWSA convention in the November 10, 1892 issue of *The People's Journal*: "The New York State Woman Suffrage Association will hold its twenty-fourth annual convention in Weiting Opera House, Syracuse, Nov. 14, 15, 16, 1892. A full attendance of delegates and friends of the Equal Suffrage cause from all parts of the state is desired. Four delegates from the Washington Co. Equality club will attend.....OFFICIAL NOTICE – Various articles in the public press indicate a misconception of the work of the woman suffragists of the country. A number of newspapers speak of 'The Woman Suffrage Candidate for the Presidency of the United States.' The National Association of the Woman Suffrage workers, the National [American] Woman Suffrage Association, though its work is of a political nature, is not a political party and has not nominated any candidate for the Presidency. – Rachel Foster Avery, Cor. Sec. N.A.W.S.A., November 7, 1892." [15]

The intense political nature of the work of NAWSA, NYSWSA, and the local Political Equality Clubs grew to a crescendo in the last decade of the 19th century. Even in the microcosm of small, rural Easton, the level of engagement for women suffrage was gaining in strength and momentum. *"Votes For Women"* was a rallying cry at the turn-of-the-20th century as women's suffrage stood on its own as an independent movement for gender political equality. In Easton, the PEC was in full-swing with monthly meetings, member education, fundraising, and involvement in county and state suffrage organizations, with which they showed unity of purpose. The ladies of Easton must surely have felt a profound sense of pride in the impact of their work and the womanly influence of their uniquely rural-inspired message of feminist reform.

As this article from *The People's Journal* on February 26, 1902 shows, the Easton PEC had grown in membership by 1900 and was focusing locally, regionally, and even internationally on the suffrage cause; and, its respected president, Lucy Allen, had become president of the Washington County Woman Suffrage Association: "Wednesday the Political Equality Club of Easton met with Mrs. Cornelius Kipp with 28 present. After a bounteous dinner the business meeting was called to order by the county president, Lucy P. Allen. The treasurer reported $13.93 on hand. Corresponding secretary reported that $2 had been sent to Miss [Harriet May] Mills as directed towards the newsletter. Mrs. Allen stated that Mrs. Fenwick Miller of England, one of their delegates to the national convention recently held in Washington, had been secured to speak at Burton Hall on Friday evening, March 7. Each paid up member will be assigned five tickets to sell at 15 cents each. The literary program was then opened with extracts from the newsletter by Mrs. Nellie Batty. The president then asked that each member be prepared at the next meeting to answer the question: 'Have you been benefitted by the P.E. club of Easton? If so, in what way, and if not, why so?' After the discussion of current events a literary program was carried out. The club now numbers 38 members with six associate members. An invitation was accepted to meet with Mrs. Hettie Snell the third Wednesday in March." [16]

This brief synopsis very fittingly portrays the flavor of the PEC meetings that took place in rural Easton.  They were held with regularity every month (despite occasional intemperate weather), and rotated among the Marshall Seminary (in the early years), Burton Hall, churches, and club members' homes.  The meetings were presided over by a slate of officers who conducted business according to parliamentary rules of order.  There was an agenda,

*Burton Hall, circa 1901*

officers gave their various reports, and certain members were appointed each month to prepare and present a paper or program on a topic of interest or relevance. Minutes were kept by a Recording Secretary and attendance was taken.

In  research for this book, PEC meeting minutes from April 1906 to January 1908, with some additional records from the years 1908, 1909, and 1910, were studied.  These documents have survived, thankfully, and are in the collection of the Easton Library.  Also in the library's collection are the PEC Yearbooks from 1908 - 1909, 1909 – 1910, and 1910 – 1911.  These small printed booklets sold for five cents and contained the names of the officers, the monthly meeting dates and program topics, inspirations, and mottoes.  To read these accounts of the busy and thought-provoking PEC gatherings is to marvel at the level of sophistication and seriousness with which they were conducted.  While socializing was indeed a part of, and a tangential purpose, of the ladies' political club, the central focus was always suffrage work and the related education and training necessary for the members to participate in their cause in the most effective manner possible.

The meeting minutes book from 1906 – 1910 is worn, but in acceptable condition.  It exists in the form of an ordinary lined composition book that might well have been for sale at any local general store in town.  Its cover is a pale pink, faded over time, with some torn edges, but the original cover decoration -- of a lady and man ice skating -- is still charmingly obvious.  The inside of the thick notebook contains the precise and exquisite penmanship of years of diligent secretaries, whose hands took care to document the PEC's proceedings with skillful accuracy and explicit detail.  Any reader of this minutes book would no doubt experience a tingle just to hold this antiquarian treasure in his or her hands and feel transported back in time to the kitchens or parlors of rural Easton farmhouses filled with dozens of conscientious women who internalized their dual roles as farm wives and rural ladies, and who knew full well that their equality as political citizens in society was an imperative and worthy goal.

The first pages of the minutes book are a listing of the 1906 – 1907 membership of the PEC:

"Mrs. Lucy P. Allen
Miss Anna B. Allen
Mrs. Lydia Batty
Mrs. Nellie Batty
Mrs. Emma Becker
Mrs. Alice Becker
Mrs. Alma Case
Mrs. Mary Brayton
Mrs. Josephine Brownell
Mrs. Julia A. Baker
Mrs. Sarah Conklin
Miss Mary Eddy
Mrs. Lydia Hoag
Miss Phebe Hoag
Mrs. Izetta Kipp
Mrs. Addie Myers

Mrs. Phebe Phillips
Mrs. Mary A. V. Sprague
Mrs. Anna E. Stiles
Mrs. Celestia Slocum
Mrs. Hetty Snell
Mrs. Chloe A. Sisson
Mrs. Sophia Sisson
Mrs. Mary L. Taylor
Mrs. Fanny Thompson
Miss Ruth Thomas
Mrs. Phebe Thomas
Miss Abbie Thomas
Mrs. Margaret M. Borden
Mrs. Ida A. Sheldon
Mrs. Anna Frisbee
Etta Lawrence


"Associate Members 1906 – 1907

Charles A. Wilbur
Mrs. J.E. Becker
Mary Wilbur
J.E. Hoag
Albert Slocum
Thomas Brownell
Harry S. Benson
Harris G. Snell
Mary A. Potter
Fred A. Laylor
Mary A. Batty" [17]

(Note the names of some men among the Associate members!)

The following newspaper clipping from *The People's Journal* of May 1906 is tucked in the early pages of the composition book:

"Suffragists' Annual Convention – The 16th annual convention of the Washington County Political Equality Club was held in the Reformed church at Greenwich on Thursday, May 16. The church had been tastefully decorated for the occasion. The word welcome made on small flags was draped over the pulpit.

"The convention was called to order by the president, Mrs. Lucy P.

Allen, with the Lord's prayer in unison. The address of welcome given by the president of the North Easton Study Club, Mrs. Carver Rice, responded to by Mrs. Allen, both in happy strain, clear, concise and to the point. Next came the reports; first that of the secretary, next of the treasury of $13.09 on hand. Work Among Young People was given by Mrs. Alice Becker; School Suffrage, Mrs. Chloe Sisson; Press Work, Mrs. Emma Becker; report of the North Easton Club, Mrs. Anna Hill; Easton club, Miss Mary Eddy; White Creek club, Mrs. Regina Thomas; West Hebron club not received. A motion prevailed for the acceptance of these reports. A letter was read from the state president, Mrs. Crossett, which was full of encouragement and commendation. A motion also prevailed for the corresponding secretary to send a letter of greeting to Mrs. Mary Hubbard, Cambridge; Mrs. Chloe Sisson, Easton; Mrs. Kenyon, Mrs. Thomas, White Creek, and Mrs. Emma Hayes of West Hebron, all valued workers who had been unable to meet with us. A pledge of $10 was made for state work and of $50 and as much more as possible to be raised for the Anthony fund. Mrs. Allen was deputed to respond to Mrs. Crossett's letter.

"Rev. Anna Howard Shaw, who had just arrived, was introduced and gave a bright sketch of the work in various parts of the country; afterwards taking charge of the question box, explaining and answering in a most delightful way all that were presented to her.

"Next followed the election of county officers with the following results: President, Mrs. Lucy P. Allen, Easton; honorary president, Mrs. Mary D. Hubbard, Cambridge; Mrs. Chloe Sisson, Easton; vice presidents, the local presidents of the county; recording secretary, Mrs. Jennie Whelden, Greenwich; corresponding secretary, Miss Mary Eddy, Easton; treasurer, Mrs. John Wilson, Greenwich.

"In the evening, ex-Assemblyman Hobbie made an address, followed by prayer. Miss Shaw then addressed the convention for the rest of the evening, holding their undivided attention. Thus has closed and entered on record one more successful convention, widening the circle each year until victory is sounded throughout the nation. – E.S. Becker, Supt. Of Press Work." [18]

Note the mention of the appearance of Reverend Dr. Anna Howard Shaw, the then-President of NAWSA, who was a motivating orator, as well as a beloved mentor to the Easton PEC and clubs throughout Washington County.

Month after month, the minutes of the Easton club illuminated the comprehensive approach the club members took to their regular gatherings. They were strict and disciplined in their agendas, with opportunities for all members to participate, whether through serving as an officer, hosting the meeting, providing refreshments, reciting a poem or devotional, presenting a report, or performing a sketch. There is no doubt that the importance placed on convening for their suffrage work was augmented by another noble purpose: education in history, current events and civics, great books and literature, and culture. From the farmhouses of Easton, the insatiable appetites of the PEC members for intellectual stimulation and knowledge were being quenched. In addition, the responsibility they assumed for educating and nurturing one another as political citizens and well-informed women reveals how dedicated they were to each other as they worked in pursuit of the suffrage cause.

A glimpse into the actual written accounts of the meetings (1906 to 1910) shows the structure and flavor of the PEC assemblies. The language used in them supports the very fundamental grounding of the members in their ladylike, feminine sphere. By the standards of late 19th century Victorian expression, the PEC meeting minutes were eloquently and intelligently rendered, and were in proper form.

Here are some representative excerpts from meeting minutes from the 1906 – 1910 period:

"[The Easton PEC] met on June 27, 1906 with Mrs. Alice Becker with 25 in attendance. The Lord's Prayer was said in unison. Mrs. Emma Becker read a poem, 'Bringing Over Sheares With Us.' Current events [were discussed]. Miss Eddy gave an account of suffrage work. Mrs. Sisson gave an account of the Oregon campaigning and the result of Sen. Brackett [of New York State] voting for the passage of the bill in regard to the right of taxpaying women to vote. An article on the eruption of Mt. Vesuvius was read by Anna Allen [daughter of Lucy Allen]. A sketch was given of Robert Burns' poem, 'To Mary In Heaven.' Mrs. Allen and Anna sang. Mrs. Addie Myers read a sketch about San Francisco since the earthquake. A sketch of the annual DAR [Daughters of the American Revolution] meeting in May in Washington was given by Mrs. Allen. Mrs. Phillips kindly gave us 'Knee Deep in June' which was very much enjoyed. Much talk on the Beef Scandal. The President [Miss Sprague] asked members to come prepared on the subject of beef raising for profit in Washington County for the next meeting. Also to learn as much as possible about the cost and purpose of the Barge Canal. – Emma Skiff Becker, Recording Secretary." [19]

"The Easton PEC met with Mrs. Phebe Phillips on July 18 [1906] with 18 in attendance. The meeting was called to order by County President Lucy P. Allen. A song by Mrs. Allen and Anna was followed by the Lord's Prayer. Mrs. Allen read a selection from 'The Mask of the Gods,' by Bayard Taylor. The minutes of the last meeting were read. The subject of short vacation trips was taken up. Miss Nellie Batty read an article – 'In Northern New York.' Miss Anna Allen gave an interesting account of some of the customs of Connecticut at a summer resort. Mrs. Lucy Allen described some Pennsylvania customs. Mrs. Chloe Sisson gave suffrage notes. Items of Work Among the Young People was given by Mrs. Alice Becker. It was moved and carried that this club offer a $3 prize for the best essay on woman's suffrage written by anyone of school age. Mrs. Fanny Thompson read an article – 'Women Voters and the Children.' Mrs. Anna Stiles read 'Women and the P.O. [Post Office]. An invitation for the August meeting was made by Izetta Kipp. An invitation for the September meeting was made by Mary Batty. Lucy and Anna pleasingly rendered another song. Mr. Boughton [unidentified] of Troy spoke a few words of approval [of suffrage]. – Emma Skiff Becker, Recording Secretary." [20]

"The Easton PEC met on August 15, 1906 with Izetta Kipp with 14 present.  First Vice President Mrs. Celestia Slocum was in charge.  A devotional poem – 'Listen for God' was read.  There are 22 paid members and $22.31 in the Treasury.  The subject of sending The Woman's Journal [a national suffrage publication] to the [Burton] Library [which pre-dated the Easton Library] - [was discussed].  There was discussion to ask the Book Committee to purchase 'The Life of Susan B. Anthony' for the Burton Library before Feb. 15, 1906.  [Susan B. Anthony had passed away earlier that year, on March 13, 1906.]  A committee was formed to arrange for flowers in case of need for members and their families.  A report of school elections was given by Mrs. Chloe Sisson.  A note of thanks was tendered to Mrs. Stiles and her daughter Mary Taylor for collecting and arranging flowers for expressions of respect on the occasion of [fellow member] Mrs. Lydia Hoag's funeral.  Resolutions of respect and esteem for Mrs. Hoag were read by Mrs. Sisson:  'In all the days of sorrow and loneliness, we trust you [PEC members] will be comforted by your unfaltering faith in the Eternal Goodness of Lydia M. Hoag.  This Society has lost a loyal member who for fifteen years has by her example and influence and her generous aid in every emergency been one of its most devoted advocates.  She recognized that Political Equality is fundamental to all reformers in that it will give woman a leverage without which most of her efforts must always be ineffective, and she was fearless in the expression of her opinions.  The Easton PEC records its respect and admiration for her life, and its sorrow and sense of loss in her death.'  The idea to present her [Lydia Hoag's] club membership to her daughter Mrs. Mary Wood Hoag [was discussed].  A decision was made to have the Corresponding Secretary write to the nominees for Congressman, Assemblyman, and Senator to ascertain their positions on the question of suffrage for women.  A paper on the Chicago campaigns for suffrage was read by Mrs. Slocum.  A sketch on the life of [national] suffragist Lucy Stone was read.  The poem, 'The Pioneers,' was read by Mrs. Sophia Sisson.  Sketches on the International League of Women Suffragists – in session in Copenhagen, Denmark – was read, followed by International Council [for Women's Suffrage] notes in Paris, which were of considerable interest.

Adjournment was followed by a luncheon. – Emma Skiff Becker, Secretary." [21]

"The Easton PEC met on September 19, 1906 with Misses Batty with 19 members and 10 visitors. There was discussion of delegates to the State Convention in Syracuse with the Club to pay expenses. There was a report on the International [Woman Suffrage] Conference in Copenhagen, Denmark. A description was given of Denmark and her people, buildings, and [author] Hans Christian Anderson. There was discussion to pay for expenses to buy the report of the [National] American Woman Suffrage Association from 1900 to 1906 for the library. Phebe Hoag read letters from [Congressional, Assembly, and Senate] nominees expressing favorable views on Woman Suffrage. The literary program was on James Russell Lowell – 'The Heritage' was read by Sophia Sisson. Adjournment was followed by lunch and a social hour. – Emma Skiff Becker, Recording Secretary." [22]

"The Easton PEC met on October 24, 1906 with 21 present at Miss Sprague's [president]. A devotional poem was read. Letters from political nominees were read – carefully worded leaving no doubt as to their [favorable] attitude toward the subject [of women's suffrage]. Mrs. Myers gave a report on the State Convention in Syracuse. A humorous sketch was read. A very entertaining and instructive paper was listened to by the club members on the teaching of young children to memorize poetry. The subject for the November meeting – 'Our Country 100 Years Ago.'" [23]

"The Easton PEC met on Wednesday, November 21 at Miss Addie Myers with 18 and unceasing rain. A devotional poem was read. 'The Delectable Mountains' was read. $15.87 is in the Treasury. There was discussion about the best ways to secure new [PEC] members – an account of how this is done in England was given. The Literary Program was 'Our Country 100 Years Ago.' Mrs. Alice Becker described the Burr-Hamilton duel." [24]

"The Easton PEC met on December 18, 1906 at Misses Lydia and Nellie Batty with 20 present. Miss Ann Batty played a piano solo. The Lord's Prayer was said in unison. A poem for the suffragettes was read by Mrs. Phillips. There was a decision to discuss taxation in Easton. The literary program was on James Madison by Mrs. Kipp. A sketch on the War of 1812 was read by Mrs. Lucy P. Allen, [there were] programs on The Star-Spangled Banner, Francis Scott Key, and Dolley Madison. Mrs. Ida Sheldon was welcomed as a new member."[25]

"The first meeting of 1907 was held on January 26, and an announcement was made of the death of member Mrs. Harriet Vanden. Sophia Sisson was asked to write a letter of condolences on behalf of the club to Mrs. Alice Becker on the loss of her sister. Professor Rosebrush [unidentified] entertained the ladies with a trombone solo, and later sang a duet with Lucy Allen. The main business of this first meeting of the year was to adopt this Resolution to be sent to the State Capitol in Albany: 'Resolved that we earnestly urge the Governor, Lieutenant Governor, Speaker of the House, Chairman of the Senate, and Assembly Judiciary Committee, the Senator and Assemblyman from this district to use their influence for the concurrent Resolution to amend the State Constitution by striking out the word 'male' which is now before the committees, and was signed by the Club and forwarded by the Corresponding Secretary."[26]

The eyes of the ladies of Easton were on the happenings in Albany, as seen above, as well as on the national suffrage stage, as seen in the February 20 meeting, at which a recently-delivered address by Reverend Dr. Anna Howard Shaw was read. Also at that meeting, a report of the funeral of Mary Anthony, sister of Susan, and the original guiding force behind the creation of the Easton PEC, was given.[27]

A lovely tribute to Mary was prepared by Chloe Sisson and adopted as a Resolution at the following month's meeting on March 21: "Whereas the Easton PEC owes a peculiar [particular] debt to Mary S. Anthony, she breathed into it the breath of life, fostered, and worshipped it through infancy and childhood, in fact prepared the ground for it years previously when a teacher of our schools, and throughout its sixteen years of effort has been an inspiration. Therefore: Be It Resolved – That we recall with deep feeling and fond pride that Mary S. Anthony's early life belonged to Washington County – that in our own town her personality left its impress, and in honor of her memory we hereby renew our fealty to the cause of our enfranchised womanhood and pledge our best efforts to help carry on the work for which she so devoted[ly]labored." [28]

The meeting on May 14, 1907 focused on a discussion of a new PEC constitution and by-laws for the club. [29] Although these documents seem not to have survived to the present day, the minutes confirm that the new constitution and by-laws were, in fact, adopted the following month at the June 15 meeting. Also at this meeting, announcement was made of auditors to examine the club's books in July.[30] It is certainly evident that the PEC officers and members were meticulous and thorough in their organization and recordkeeping, and that they conducted their business with the utmost honesty and integrity.

New PEC officers were chosen in the summer of 1907 and a review of the minutes shows the slate of the new leaders, along with a listing of the various club committees and their chairwomen. The standing committees were: Membership, Enrollment, Press, Foreign Affairs, Home Affairs, Flowers, Resolutions, Work Among Young People, Programs (Literary, Suffrage), and Parliamentarian. Such an elaborate organization of functions supports the fact that the PEC took seriously its mission at home and beyond, its duty to its fellow members and the young citizens of Easton, recruitment, and judicious management of the civic and financial responsibilities of the club. [31]

The September 18, 1907 meeting included a discussion of ways to further extend the work of the PEC and to make its influence felt to a greater degree in the town. Also, Mrs. Celestia Slocum was selected as the Easton PEC's delegate to the State Woman Suffrage Convention in Geneva, New York in October. Chloe Sisson conducted a parliamentary drill lasting fifteen minutes on the subject of making motions, which invoked much amusement. A motion was carried at this meeting to investigate the organization of the Grange and to see if one could be established in Easton. And, in keeping with the ladies' interest in the suffrage cause around the world, the members were read a report about the imprisonment of seventy English suffragettes. [32]

More talk on the Grange question continued into the fall of 1907, along with inspiration from state and national figures who lent their encouragement and support to Easton's work. An inspiring word of sentiments from renowed suffrage leader Elizabeth Cady Stanton was shared at the November 20 meeting, along with a letter from State Assembly candidate, James S. Parker, promising to do his utmost for the cause should he be elected Assemblyman. [33]

The influence of the PEC was shown in full force at the January 1908 meeting when an announcement was made of the establishment of the Easton Grange. The minutes read: "Due credit was taken by the Club for introducing the Grange question in the community in order to widen our sphere of usefulness in the town." [34] The Grange was formed with thirty-four members, many of them also PEC members and their husbands, and continued to be active in Easton for many years.

Even into the summer of 1908, the PEC stayed strong in its commitment to suffrage education and in supporting the Easton community and its newest institution. The August 19 meeting included a discussion of why the farmers of the town should join the Grange. This business was followed by the reading of a letter by Lucy Allen from the president of the woman suffrage association in England, and a letter was read by Miss Eddy from new NAWSA President, Carrie Chapman Catt. [35]

By 1908, the ladies were busy supporting the establishment of PECs in nearby towns – including Sandy Hill in Washington County and neighboring Valley Falls in Rensselaer County, which hosted the County women's suffrage convention on September 20, 1908. [36]

Never losing their priority and pride in family life, the ladies, at the

October 21 meeting, presented their fellow member, Sophia Sisson, with a handsome "baby sack" for her newborn son. This note accompanied the gift:

> "To your little man-cub,
> Welcome from the PEC Club.
> 'Ere he needs a grown-up coat,
> May his mother have a vote."

A note of thanks from the baby, George W. Sisson, was also shared:

> "To the PEC Club
> Thank you for your welcome
> And the pretty woolen coat.
> When I get to be a man
> I'll see to it that women vote! [37]

The suffrage program at this meeting was entitled "Working Women and the Ballot," and the literary program was "Finland and Its People" and "Woman's Part in Finland's Freedom." [38]  Once again, each PEC meeting was an intentional blend of work for suffrage at home, education, world and cultural awareness, and feminine hobbies and interests – and always a musical interlude.

At the November 18, 1908 meeting, Miss Sprague gave a synopsis of the twenty years succeeding the Seneca Falls [women's rights] convention, and she and Lucy Allen gave an account of the National Convention they had recently attended in Buffalo, New York.  The minutes of December 15 report that "Roll call was responded to by stating why we are all suffragists" and "a motion was carried that the PEC should subscribe to the English Suffrage Paper." In addition, "an answer to [President Theodore] Roosevelt's letter on behalf of woman suffrage written by the President of the Troy [in New York] [Political Equality] Club was read." The literary topic of the month was "The Hudson River." [39]

Programs on national suffragists like Elizabeth Cady Stanton, Lucretia Mott, and Lucy Stone were offered in 1909, and the PEC members continued their education on suffrage topics like "Unjust Laws for Women." [40]

As the winds of war were blustering in Europe, the ladies of Easton turned to topics of world peace and debate on military engagement by the United States. At the PEC meeting on May 19, 1909, held at the Easton Grange Hall, the following program topics were presented: "Furtherance of the Peace Cause," "Why Our Navy Should Not Be Engaged," Women on Civil Service," "White Slave Trade," and "Needless Expenditures of the Navy." In addition, an original paper on "Pioneer Women" was presented by Chloe Sisson. [41]

Throughout the summer of 1909, the club continued fundraising for its suffrage work, including selling ice cream at the Grange picnic to cover expenses for sending delegates to the Troy Convention in October. [42] Discussions on "how to introduce more suffrage sentiment into the local temperance union," juvenile courts, treatment of child offenders, and child labor were held, along with literary programs on "Our Native Birds," "What the Birds Say," and Samuel de Champlain." The ladies held their own debate, articulating opposing views in "Why Women Should and Should Not Vote." [43]

New members were constantly being added and rejoiced in, as this notation from the August 18, 1909 meeting read in welcoming Sarah Pimlott and Lucy Brownell: "The Club extends to them the same cordial welcome that it does to all who join our ranks." [44]

By the fall of 1909, discussions were being held about the "advisability" of joining the State Federation of Clubs, an offshoot of the national organization of the same name that promoted club membership, leadership, and volunteerism among women. The goal of continuing cooperation with the local temperance union was also reintroduced at the October 29 meeting with this mention: "There was a discussion of franchise work in the WCTU, which has sadly been neglected." [45]

Members Sophia Sisson and Alice Becker traveled to the northern part of Washington County – to the Whitehall Grange – in December 1909 to promote the women's suffrage cause among the community members there, and they reported back to Easton at the monthly meeting on the 15th. Also at this meeting, "Mr. Pimlott [husband of new member Sarah Pimlott] gave a fine talk on suffrage, also suggesting ways to advance the cause, then showing that he is decidedly in favor of women having the franchise."[46]

The meetings of early 1910 saw a renewed effort to lobby the New York State legislature for the removal of the word *male* in the State Constitution. The various PECs in Washington County joined together in adopting and presenting a resolution on this. And, as always, suffrage programs like "The Power of the Ballot" and "Votes for Women" were intermingled with topics like "How to Cook a Chicken" and "Resolved: That a Garden is More Care Than Profit to a Farmer's Wife." The charming duality of conscientious civic education with the furtherance of domestic skills – without compromising the strength of their commitment to either mission – was a constant feature of PEC gatherings.[47]

The use of letterwriting and petitioning the government, commonly used methods by the Easton PEC, saw a new target of expression in the Woman Suffrage Protest Meeting which was held in Union Square in New York City on Saturday, May 21, 1910 at 3:30 in the afternoon. The purpose was to protest the actions of the New York State legislature in obstructing gender neutral language in the State Constitution and, more generally, the cause of female enfranchisement. One of the chief organizers of this event was Harriot Stanton Blatch, daughter of Elizabeth Cady Stanton, who, by 1910, had become a major figure in the national suffrage movement. Blatch successfully understood the need to broaden the base of involvement for women's suffrage to young working women and immigrants, and she energized a new generation of suffrage advocates. The ladies of Easton discussed this dynamic suffragist at their May 10 meeting, and "yellow slips" were distributed on which the members were urged to obtain signatures on behalf of the protest. A notice of the protest meeting was tucked into the minutes book from this May meeting, and new member Mrs. Ora R. Anthony was made the delegate to the protest meeting from Easton.[48]

The minutes book continued with reports through 1910 and 1911, reporting on fundraising, letterwriting to state representatives, initiatives with other county PECs, and suffrage education. By 1911, it is evident that the focus of the club on its mission of suffrage while embracing the domestic sphere remained paramount. The program, "An Educational Qualification for Suffrage Is the Most Imperative for Reform" on April 19 [49] was followed by a program on "Sentiments on Housecleaning" on May 17. [50] On June 21, it was reported that devoted member Hetty Snell had died; the topics for this meeting were "Home Economics" and "The Growth of the Baby." [51]

Minutes from the remainder of 1911 and to the conclusion of the paperbound composition book told of suffrage debates at Burton Hall and the Easton Grange, and mention resolutions prepared by PEC officers in furtherance of female enfranchisement in New York.

The final meeting in this only remaining document of the Easton PEC is from August 16, 1911. Very aptly, and underscoring the bonds between the women, "Sentiments on Friendship" was read after the roll call. Also, Lucy Allen read a letter from [the state suffrage coordinator] "Miss [Harriet May] Mills enthusiastically reviewing the summer campaign of suffragists who toured through northern New York." The literary program was "Clara Barton." And, in a display (once again) of the nurturing and caring among the ladies of the PEC, "a motion was made by Mrs. Taylor that Mrs. Sisson and Miss Eddy be sent to Lake George [in the Adirondacks, in northern New York] for a vacation of three weeks, the Club to pay expenses."[52]

A January 3, 1912 article in *The Greenwich Journal* showed that twenty-one years after its founding the Easton Political Equality Club was still going strong – and still working in cooperation with the local chapter of the Women's Christian Temperance Union: "The W.C.T.U. and Political Equality club met in joint session at the home of Mr. and Mrs. Charles Case on Wednesday, December 27th from 10 a.m. to 4 p.m. A very fine dinner was served by the ladies. A varied program was given by the two societies which was a very interesting one, with musical selections interspersed between. The talk by Miss

Sprague was unusually entertaining and instructive, considerable business was agitated by both societies. Suffrage notes and current events were given. Christmas and New Year sentiments were given in response to roll call. A very large number were in attendance and the meeting was a great success." [53]

Two weeks later, the PEC met at Lucy Allen's house: "The Political Equality club met Saturday afternoon with Mrs. Lucy P. Allen and daughter, Anna, with a very good attendance. Current events and home and foreign affairs were given by members. Several songs were given by the club. Miss Sprague took the topic of the day, "Charles Dickens," handling it in a very pleasing and interesting manner. Mrs. Phebe Deuel took the question, "How may we best simplify the methods of housekeeping," which received discussion from every member present. Mrs. Sophia Sisson read an article from Henry Thoreau on that subject. The program was followed by a social hour during which refreshments were served. It was decided to send a box of canned fruit to New York City as Easton's contribution to the suffrage fair to be held there. A play by local talent will be given during February for the benefit of the club. The President, Mrs. Alice Becker, appointed Miss Sprague, Mrs. Sisson, and Miss Allen a committee on a guessing contest. Members are requested to submit lists of names of the 25 greatest women in history. Women on the lists must be chosen because of essential greatness, not fame. The club adjourned to meet in Burton Hall in February." [54]

The ties between Easton and the Washington County branch of the New York State Woman Suffrage Association were strong from the 1890's into the first two decades of the 1900's. As early as 1894, three years after the establishment of the Easton club, three of the four officers of the county PEC hailed from Easton: Chloe Sisson, President; Julia Baker, Corresponding Secretary; and Celestia Slocum, Treasurer. Later, Lucy Allen served as county president for many years. The development and growth of other PECs in Washington County in the period 1891 – 1916 -- Granville, Shushan, Greenwich, Cambridge, Hebron, White Creek, Hudson Falls (Sandy

Hill), and Fort Edward – was largely due to the early example and influence of the lady leaders of Easton.

Newspaper coverage of the activities of the Easton PEC continued even after female enfranchisement was won in New York in 1917. The club altered its focus from the ballot to citizenship education. A March 20, 1918 article in *The Greenwich Journal* announced a PEC meeting in which "lessons in civics will be continued. All interested are invited to attend." [55]  On August 28, 1918, this article appeared, mentioning "a political mass meeting at Burton Hall, Easton [will be held] under the auspices of the Easton PEC. The candidates for member of assembly are expected to be present, and everybody is invited." [56]  *The Greenwich Journal* reported on women voting for the first time in "several local option propositions" in October 1918, the same day that news of an influenza epidemic in Washington County was described.[57] Even into the early 1920's, after the franchise for women was won nationwide, the PEC continued to meet and to sponsor worthwhile public programs about political issues and candidates, and to educate the community about civics and the workings of government.

With their work done, however, the PEC members searched for and found a new focus: books and reading. The great literary programs that had always been a feature of the monthly gatherings became a mission unto themselves. The companionship, socializing, and intellectual stimulation that the ladies of Easton had nurtured and enjoyed among themselves over three decades found a new outlet. On September 26, 1926, the Easton Book Club was organized at the home of Sophia Sisson for the purpose of "reading and reviewing worthwhile books." [58] This club is still in existence today.

Over the years, the inspirations and mottoes for the suffrage work of the Easton PEC remained firmly rooted in the twin goals of legitimacy and value of the role of women in political life and in the domestic sphere. In 1908 – 1909, the club's motto as it appeared in its yearbook was "The Justice of Our Cause," and its inspiration was Susan B. Anthony's battle cry, "Failure is Impossible." [59]   The yearbook in 1910 – 1911 offered this motivating quote from Reverend Charles Aked to the ladies: "Nothing since the coming of Christ ever promised so much for the ultimate good of the human race as the intellectual, moral, and political emancipation of women." [60] In 1918, the year after victory in New York for votes for women, the yearbook's motto was: "For God, For Home, for Every Land." [61]

Having achieved success for their noble cause, the ladies of Easton transformed their group from one dedicated to obtaining political equality with men to furthering the intellectual advancement of women. Just as the bonds of sisterhood and friendship had energized and propelled the PEC members toward their goal by 1917, so they continued, in creating a base of active participation in the various organizations of the town – like the Book Club, and the Grange. The magic of *womanly influence*, combined with a commitment to each other and to their community, earned the ladies of the Easton Political Equality Club a well-deserved place in the history of women's suffrage in rural upstate New York.

# Chapter V

## Easton Suffragists:
## Lucy Allen and Chloe Sisson

Much has been written about the partnership and friendship of national suffrage pioneers, Susan B. Anthony and Elizabeth Cady Stanton, but the duo of Lucy Allen and Chloe Sisson was a collaboration of significant import regionally, in rural upstate New York. Through their writings, papers, and correspondence, their characters and commitment to the cause – along with their genuine fondness for one another – is revealed. Individually, Lucy and Chloe brought great enthusiasm and verve to the Easton PEC; as a team, they left a lasting legacy. As friends, neighbors, and co-leaders of the local suffrage club, these two women demonstrated the power of articulate written expression which, when coupled with effective organization, made success for suffrage a reality.

Lucy Phillips Allen was born in Pennsylvania in 1851 and was educated (and later taught in) a girls' boarding school there. [1] She moved to Easton in 1876 with her family to teach at Friends' Seminary where, on Friday evenings, public programs and debates on current events were held. In Lucy's own words: "First the students entertained with declamations, compositions, and so forth.

*Lucy Allen, circa 1910*

Then the time was given to the debaters.  Prominent among these were Frederick Ives, Lewis Potter, Joseph Peckham, the Borden boys, Warren Fort, Jonathan Hoag, the Woods, the Sissons, and many others.  No question before the State Legislature, before Congress, or before the world was too great for these debaters to tackle.  Woman Suffrage and Temperance were never-ending topics.  And how the people came to these gatherings!  Every inch of space in schoolroom, class room, hall, and stairways was filled.  I do not know who first suggested that an admission of ten cents be charged for all not connected with the school, the money to go toward a library.  It was so decided – and still the people came.  Miss Mitchell and I often found one dollar bills among the ten cent collections.  The first $100 for our library was raised this way." [2]  This was how Lucy Allen became one of the founders of the first library in Easton.  The library was chartered in 1895 and was located in Burton Hall (across from the current Easton Library) from 1902 to 1955. [3]  This was only the beginning of her magnificent touch in influencing culture and people in her new hometown.

Lucy Allen went on to be active in many local organizations in addition to the library – including the formation of the Political Equality Club (PEC), the Grange, and the Easton Book Club.  Lucy married George S. Allen, of Easton, and they were the parents of Anna Allen, who later would become Anna A. Pratt, and who was herself active in the PEC.  Anna, along with Chloe Sisson, wrote a description of the suffrage club for the 1959 *History of Washington County*. [4]

The friendship and mutual admiration between Lucy Allen and Chloe Sisson began as soon as young Lucy moved to town in 1876.  In the obituary that Lucy wrote for her dear friend in 1923, she recalled: "We came to Easton in December 1876, a stranger in a strange land.  Mrs. Sisson and her family took us in.  Then began a friendship that has grown sweeter with each passing year.  Such a friend as remembers us when we have forgotten ourselves; such a friend as takes loving heed of our health, our work, our aims, our plans.  It takes a great soul to be a true friend, a large, steadfast, and loving spirit.  No doubts, no misunderstandings have ever come to vex our place." [5]

Not only is this passage a testament to the tender bond of Mrs. Allen and Mrs. Sisson, but it is also a telltale example of the eloquence of Lucy's writing talents, which found an important outlet in the work of the Easton PEC. Both Chloe and Lucy were excellent and articulate writers, constantly demonstrating creative and prolific skill in bringing forth the message and goal of women's suffrage to the townspeople of Easton and to the residents of Washington County.

*Chloe Sisson, circa 1880*

Ten years older than Lucy, Chloe Sisson was born in 1841, the daughter of Joseph W. and Elizabeth Gifford Peckham.  She married William B. Sisson on November 10, 1869, and they had two children, Burton and Mabel.  Burton's wife, Sophia, was an active member of the PEC.  The elegantly penned obituary of Mrs. Sisson by her friend Lucy Allen described a life of great influence in the Easton area:

" Those friends who were privileged to look, for the last time, upon the earthly form of Mrs. Sisson were touched by the saintliness of her face.  She looked as though pain and fear and doubt had never troubled her, as though she had let go of all unworthy things, pretense, worry, discontent, self-seeking, and had taken loyal hold of happiness, love, duty, and faith. One felt that her courageous spirit, as of old still marched 'breast forward, held we fall to rise, are baffled to fight better, sleep to wake.'

"Such a transition is not a thing for sorrow, rather for rejoicing.

"Mrs. Sisson was educated in the schools of Easton. She attended for a time a private school taught by Mary Anthony, sister of Susan B. Anthony, in the house now owned by Moses Charbeauneau. She said in after [later] life that what she had gained at this private school meant more to her than all she had gained before. Afterwards she attended Albany State Normal School, where she was graduated July 11, 1861. Here she came to know the Powell family – Elizabeth Powell Bond, ex-dean of Swarthmore College, was her classmate and friend.

"Mrs. Sisson's parents were deeply interested in the Abolition movement and her home became a resting place for many weary anti-slavery reformers, when their speaking tours about the county brought them near. Thus she became acquainted with such men as Charles G. Ames, Charles C. Burleigh, William Lloyd Garrison, Parker Pillsbury, Aaron M. Powell and others. These great and good men with their hatred of wrong, their love of justice, their integrity and truthfulness, found rich and fertile soil in the mind of this young woman wherein to plant their principles.

"We, who have heard her speak of them, will long remember her happiness in recalling to memory this time in her girlhood, and will understand the inspiration that came to her from this association.

"After graduation, Mrs. Sisson spent some years teaching, principally in the towns of Easton and White Creek. [.....]

"October 10, 1891, at the earnest solicitation of Miss Mary Anthony, Mrs. Sisson organized the Easton Political Equality Club with eight charter members. Even at this late date, suffrage workers were abused, maligned, and misrepresented. Mrs. Sisson was brave. She feared nobody and nothing except wrong doing. Those who worked with her came to know the beauty and nobility of her character. During the life of this club, until its goal was reached and the vote won, she was its chief inspiration, counselor, and guide." [6]

Clearly, the affection of the two women grew from the early years of their acquaintanceship as mothers and wives in Easton to their co-founding and leadership of the PEC. Interestingly, while Lucy Allen had the more visible leadership roles over the years – both in the local club and in county work – she wrote and acted in deference to her older, esteemed friend, Chloe Sisson, who was more comfortable behind the scenes.

*Chloe Sisson, circa 1920*

This glowing tribute to Chloe's talents was written by Lucy as she described a meeting of the Washington County women's suffrage club: "I was struck dumb by the amount of information, the enthusiasm, and the high literary excellence displayed in the papers read. It was some time afterwards that I learned that Mrs. Sisson was the author or the compiler of every paper read that afternoon."[7] Lucy went on to praise their Easton PEC: "I think this is a remarkable record of work for a little county club. I well remember the first state convention I attended – where I learned to love and respect our Easton club more than I had before. A little band of women apparently cherishing a forlorn hope, ridiculed and condemned by the majority yet striving 'To strive, to seek, to find and not to yield.' I learned there that [the] Easton Club had a record of faithfulness, devotion, [and] hard work."[8]

Also among the papers of Lucy Allen is a handwritten letter from Chloe Sisson, penned on February 27, 1923 (when Chloe was nearing the age of eighty-two) as Lucy and her husband prepared to retire and move away from Easton:

"My dear Mrs. Allen,

"Since I cannot see you, I feel that I must write a few lines that you may know how much I regret that you are making this change, tho it is in my selfishness that I am so sorry to have you any farther away that you can no longer be able to walk over, that I can only see you less and less often.

"Your companionship and neighborliness has been so much more to me than you can realize, especially since, as much of a shut-in, I have greatly missed your cheering calls. While I am glad that both you and George can be released from the care and work of farm life, and hope for you a comfortable old age.

"With best wishes and love, ever your friend,
                    Chloe A. Sisson." [9]

Chloe Sisson died in December 1923, ten months after writing this heartfelt note to her lifelong friend. It is fascinating to contemplate the sweet, yet sad, goodbye of these two women who had labored together for votes for women and had lived long enough to cast their ballots in the Presidential election of 1920. What satisfaction and triumph they must have felt.

Also among Lucy Allen's papers -- in the collection of the Easton Library – are mementoes of her attachment to the national suffrage movement and its leaders, Susan B. Anthony and Elizabeth Cady Stanton. There is a program from the 80th birthday celebration given by Stanton for her friend Miss Anthony on February 15, 1900, just two years before Elizabeth's death and six years before Susan's. There is the "Order of Service" from the memorial service of Susan B. Anthony, held on March 15, 1906 at Central Church in Rochester, New York, two days after her passing. Among the speakers were noted abolitionist William Lloyd Garrison, and suffrage leaders, Reverend Dr. Anna Howard Shaw and Carrie Chapman Catt. Pictures of Lucy's mentor, Susan B. Anthony, were among the papers, along with some personal letters to Lucy from Susan. Two letters date from 1900. The first is dated February 15 and reads:

"My dear friend –

"Political Equality of rights for women – civil and political – is today, and has been for the past half-century the one demand of –

"Yours sincerely
Susan B. Anthony
Rochester, N. Y." [10]

The second letter was dated April 18th and reads:

"My dear Mrs. Allen and all good friends of Easton, N.Y. –

"Your letter and check of $8 are here this morning.  The check shall be deposited in the Security First Bank where are already near $2,000 waiting for company to come.  A lady in Boston sent $1,000 the other day.  If every club would do as nicely as yours of Easton, we should soon reach a very respectable fraction of our hoped for half million!

"I remember the good old Easton Friends' Meeting House – and the good friends – the Quakers – the Hoxies, Wilburs, etc. etc.

"With many thanks and much love,
Susan B. Anthony" [11]

Lucy's certificate of a fifty dollar contribution to the treasury of the New York State Woman Suffrage Association and a life membership to it, signed by State President Harriet May Mills, has survived among her mementoes.  And, never one to lose her sentiment for her local PEC, Lucy proudly kept a gilt-papered cardboard A, cut out and covered by her mother, Mary Phillips, to spell out **POLITICAL EQUALITY CLUB** on the wall of suffrage headquarters [12] located at Aaron B. Allen's vacant store at Barker's Grove. [13]

Lucy P. Allen, who was to Easton, New York what Susan B. Anthony was to the United States, died in 1946, at the age of ninety-five.

# Chapter VI
## More Washington County Suffragists:
## Elizabeth Wakeman Mitchell and Laura Schafer Porter

The significance of friendship and mentoring between and among women in the suffrage movement contributed greatly to eventual success in reaching its goal. The historic partnership of Susan B. Anthony and Elizabeth Cady Stanton; the four-way collaboration of Anthony, Stanton, Lucretia Mott, and Lucy Stone; and the mentoring by them of a new generation of suffragists, like Harriot Stanton Blatch and Alice Paul, made for continuity and support over decades as the fight for the ballot ensued.

In addition to the figures that populated the national suffrage stage, suffrage leaders in the cities, towns, and villages across America enlivened the debate and carried forward the message and goal of the national effort down to the local and regional levels. The stories of these women are often lost in the history of the larger women's movement, and sadly so, for their contributions were legion, and their impact was decisive. Lucy Allen and Chloe Sisson of Easton, for example, typify this type of magical duo that inspired women in rural upstate New York at the turn of the 20th century. Two more women of Washington County, contemporaries of Lucy Allen and Chloe Sisson, who were suffrage leaders in nearby Hudson Falls and Fort Edward were Elizabeth Wakeman Mitchell and Laura Schafer Porter. This rural county had a well-organized and very active suffrage effort during the late 19th and early 20th centuries – even in comparison to its two neighboring counties, Warren and Saratoga, which included the cities of Glens Falls and Saratoga Springs, respectively.

In the historic villages of Hudson Falls and Fort Edward, both of which had played important roles as venues in the Revolutionary War and still have the architecture and homages to famous personages to attest to it, women's suffrage was a highly publicized matter in the first two decades of the 1900's. *The Hudson Falls Herald*, a weekly newspaper, carried many articles and cartoons pertaining to the fight for female enfranchisement. Due to the close proximity of Saratoga Springs, Glens Falls, and Albany, articles and cartoons from these larger, more urban centers also appeared in the Hudson Falls paper, giving local readers a taste of the issue as it was being debated on a wider stage.

By the time President Woodrow Wilson finally called upon Americans to support the right for women to vote in 1917, the female population was beginning to feel the burden put on them by World War I. As men left for European soil and the Pacific, American women were saddled not only with their usual domestic workload but also that of the absent male population – in factories and on farms. As such, political cartoons with strongly worded captions such as "Women Share the Hard Work; Why Not the Vote?" and "Burdens of the War; Why Not the Vote?" appeared weekly in *The Hudson Falls Herald.* [1]

Suffrage activity in Hudson Falls, in comparison to Glens Falls, for example, was much more pervasive and was characterized by a well-organized and hard-working network of women – and men – devoted to the suffrage cause. Even *The Glens Falls Times and Messenger* and *The Post Star* of Glens Falls ran daily articles on suffrage activities in neighboring Hudson Falls. [2]

By 1914, the ideas of the women's suffrage movement were regularly making the headlines in Washington County newspapers. A woman, signing herself only as a "Washington County suffragist," began writing articles to the editor of *The Hudson Falls Herald* to present her views. It seems likely that some mystery must have surrounded this anonymous figure. The July 9, 1914 issue ran the following article from her: "The 'Antis' never complain that the home is neglected because the church pews, with the possible exception of the aisle seats, are filled with women, or because they spend much time in performing charitable, or social, or business duties and seem to think it less 'womanly' to cast a vote for decent politics than to vote for missionary society president, take part in public entertainment, transact business in a bank or work in an office, where they are not always 'fed and protected' very luxuriously by the 'hand' of an employer. The average man does not neglect his business nor his family because he votes – neither would the average woman. Admitting an 'Anti' argument that the 'average woman cannot vote intelligently,' then neither can the average man." [3]

An editorial reply from the same date read: "Elsewhere we print a communication from an ardent Washington County advocate of the cause of woman suffrage. The writer, in a personal note to the editor of the *Herald*, says, that one of the reasons which compels her to present her views is that the people of the county may be more thoroughly informed regarding what she believes to be the greatest issue of the age. Her views are worth reading and, as this is another question which will undoubtedly be made the subject of a great deal of debate at the coming constitutional convention, it is well that the matter be carefully considered by people generally from every viewpoint. The *Herald* invites short articles from its readers either for or against 'votes for women.'" [4]

By 1916, articles appeared in *The Hudson Falls Herald* praising the persistency of the suffragists in their battle to win the ballot. Slogans used by the New York State Woman Suffrage Party -- such as "Eventually; Why Not Now?" -- seemed to add to the sense of urgency. A cartoon featured on June 22, 1916 pictured a nicely dressed woman standing between Charles Evans Hughes and Woodrow Wilson. The caption read simply: "The Political Debutante." Hughes and Wilson were the Presidential candidates in the 1916 election, Republican and Democrat, respectively. For this cartoon, featuring the venerable Charles Evans Hughes, to appear was of particular significance to area residents. Hughes, who later became the Chief Justice of the Supreme Court (1930 – 1941), was a native of Glens Falls. As part of his Presidential platform, he was committed to the cause of women's suffrage, and several articles about his views on this topic were printed in *The Hudson Falls Herald*. Woodrow Wilson defeated Hughes, however, and eventually did come out in support of suffrage, although that was not his original stance. [5]

Much of the excitement and support for suffrage in Hudson Falls was generated by Elizabeth Wakeman Mitchell. By 1916, it was clear that the local movement had its leader, and it was Mrs. Willis G. Mitchell. Rarely a mention of suffrage activity would appear in area newspapers without a summary of her comments or her picture. She became the powerhouse behind suffrage in Hudson Falls and in Washington County. On June 22, 1916, she was elected president of the Hudson Falls Political Equality Club. In July 1916, she became Assembly District Leader of Washington County for the New York State Woman Suffrage Party. In September 1916, she attended the 48th Annual Convention of the National American Woman Suffrage Association (NAWSA) in Atlantic City. She was also part of an entourage of suffragists that visited President Wilson at the White House to ask for his support of women's suffrage. In January 1917, she was selected as the Grange Chairman of the State suffrage party; later on, she served as the Chairman of the Endorsements Committee. In 1918, she became Chairman of the Rural Problems Committee. In April 1918, she ran for State Assemblyman from Washington County on the Republican ticket, but was defeated. [6]

Elizabeth Wakeman was born at Sandy Hill (now Hudson Falls) in 1885. She spent some of her later years in New York City, and died in 1960. As a child, Betty, as she was called, lived with her family at Springside, the Wakeman estate at 179 Main Street. Springside is today an historic landmark and contains an unusual brick basement floor and hideaway which are believed to

*Elizabeth Wakeman Mitchell*
*circa 1915*

be evidence of the house's use as a station on the "underground railroad," a legendary network of people and places assisting fugitive slaves on their way to freedom in Canada.  It is also believed that Susan B. Anthony, who taught school in the neighboring village of Fort Edward and is said to be a cousin of Betty Wakeman, may have visited Springside on a few occasions. [7]

Betty Wakeman married Willis G. Mitchell, who was a captain in the United States Navy and the chief engineer of the Atlantic fleet in World War I. [8]

Mrs. Mitchell was an energetic spokeswoman for the women's suffrage cause and had excellent organizational and fundraising abilities.   She organized card parties in the Hudson Falls-Fort Edward area in 1916 – 1917 to raise money for local suffrage activities. [9]

Like the suffragists of Easton, Elizabeth Wakeman Mitchell was proud to use her femininity in support of her cause.  First and foremost, she was a mother – of two daughters and a son.  Believing it was never too early to instill the fervor of the suffrage cause in her girls, Betty brought them – at ages four and two – with her as she toured the region while campaigning for State Assembly in 1916, with "Votes For Women" as her platform.  The following article appeared in *The Tribune* on August 29:

"Tiny Campaigners Are Winning Votes to Send Mama to Albany – Helen, Four, and Betty, Two, Stump Washington County in Interest of Mother" – With 'Vote for Mama' emblazoned across their small waists, Betty and Helen Mitchell, of Hudson Falls, of the ripe ages of two and four, have entered the primary fight as the youngest campaigners in the history of politics.  Their mother, Betty Wakeman Mitchell, is contesting with three opponents on the Republican ticket for Assemblyman from Washington County, and among all the women of the county and state who are helping her in her fight are these 'baby campaigners,' as they are called.

" It was not for nothing that Helen, the four-year-old, hit the trail for suffrage last year, and it is with the wisdom of experience, therefore, that she is now riding around in automobiles, throwing out leaflets and waving banners to 'Help Mama.' As for Betty, she hasn't quite mastered the art of stumping, so she just follows sister around, sticking out her stomach proudly with its 'Vote for Mama' sash and obediently lisping little formulas about 'keeping the home fireth burning.'

"County fairs, old home days, and all other society events of Washington County have the Mitchells on their programme these days, and though Mrs. Mitchell is making a vigorous fight and is an accomplished speaker, it is the babies who are most sought after by the countryfolk here whenever the Michell touring car comes into sight.

" 'I'm not a blonde; I'm not a brunette; I'm a suffragette.' Helen summed it up the other day to a farmer who was trying to tease her. 'My papa's away in the navy and my mama's going to be elected and go to Albany, she is.'

"Mrs. Mitchell is one of the active members of the New York State Woman Suffrage State Committee. The woman suffragists of her county are conducting a live campaign for her nomination. If she should receive it, Mrs. Mitchell will go to Albany as this is an overwhelmingly Republican district whose only contest comes in the primaries."[10]

Betty Wakeman Mitchell, even though unsuccessful in her bid for Assemblyman, actively sought to gain broad support from throughout Washington County for women's right to vote. [11] As Grange Chairman for the State suffrage party, she used the Grange as a model of a solid, rural institution, which, since its beginning, offered equal status for women. Pointing out the close association between the Grange and the suffrage movement, Betty remarked in a March 15, 1917 article in *The Hudson Falls Herald*: "We have no stronger ally in our fight for suffrage than the Grange. The farmer's wife has nobly done her work on the farm and the farming community, and the farmer is ready to show her justice by giving her a voice in the government." [12]  She also spoke out on behalf of rural nurses who worked in areas like Washington County.

By 1917, Betty was able to boast that 7,134 of the one million enrolled members of the state suffrage organization were residents of Washington County (as reported in *The Hudson Falls Herald* on October 24, 1917). She pointed out that this was more than the total enrolled members of the Democratic and Republican parties combined in the county. [13] Betty's influence was extraordinary.

Her methods included educating county residents about women's suffrage through a suffrage school, organized under the auspices of the Hudson Falls Political Equality Club, of which she was president. The "school," which consisted of a series of lectures, ran from March 20 through March 24, 1917, and was held in the Hudson Falls' library assembly room.    Beginning in January, articles appeared in the *Herald* announcing the coming "school." A January 11 article noted that 1, 049 Hudson Falls women had enrolled. [14]

Elinor Byrnes, a trained suffrage director and member of the Women's Lawyer's Association and of the New York State County Lawyers Association, conducted the suffrage school.    One period of each session was devoted to suffrage history, then the class would focus on discussions and questions.    Members of the class presented papers on topics such as:    Why Women Want to Vote, Children of the State, Progress by Suffrage, The State as a Mother, and Why the Ballot Needs a Woman.    Lectures were held on the following subjects:    History of Manhood Suffrage in the United States and England, Legal Status of Women (Old and New Laws), Publicity of Suffrage, Parliamentary Law, and Organization of an Election District.    Follow-up newspaper articles indicated that the suffrage school was very well attended. [15]

A Men's League for women's suffrage was organized in Washington County and the chairman of it was Erskine C. Rogers, of Hudson Falls. [16] The men's group wrote and spoke out in favor of the vote for women, authoring editorials in local newspapers, representing the county in suffrage parades, and distributing pro-suffrage literature.

A partner for Betty Wakeman Mitchell in county suffrage work was Laura Schafer Porter of Fort Edward, a village next door to Hudson Falls. Laura Porter was one of the original members of the Fort Edward Suffrage Club, along with Mr. and Mrs. Fred Davis, Mary Bradley, Ida May Powell, Mrs. and Mrs. Albert Wicks, and Mr. and Mrs. H. Payne, and she later became its president. [17]

In the following letter, dated September 12, 1917, Betty, in her capacity as Assembly District Leader for the State suffrage party, welcomed Laura as the new president of the Fort Edward club:

"My dear Mrs. Porter:

"You don't know how pleased I am to think that you are to be President of the Fort Edward Suffrage Club. I just feel now that if you were only going to be there through the Campaign that we would not have to worry about Fort Edward a bit.

"I have just written the enclosed letter to Mrs. Wicks [member of the local club] and am sending you a copy. I hope it meets with your approval. When I got home, I found that the envelopes were $12.40 a thousand and that, with the literature, it made $15.40 a thousand.

However, I went ahead and ordered them; if you find that it is more than you can pay, we will just have to make it up some way, if I have to get out and dig for it! If you have the card party, I am sure it will help a lot.

"Have you had a chance to see Ethel Goodfellow [a mutual friend] yet? If she will

*Laura Schafer Porter, circa 1905*

only help we will pull that district into good shape. Don't you think Mrs. Howland might give her house for a Card Party? If she only would it would make success certain; everyone would want to come just to see the house and gardens whether they play or not.

"If there is ever anything I can do to help you, do not hesitate to call on me.

"Sincerely yours,
    Betty Wakeman Mitchell
    Assembly District Leader" [18]

Laura Schafer Porter was born on October 16, 1881 and came to Fort Edward with her parents in the 1880's. She graduated from the Fort Edward Collegiate Institute, where she was trained as an artist. She taught in South Carolina and then chaired the Art Department at Brenau College in Gainsville, Georgia for ten years. She also trained as an occupational therapist and worked at Walter Reed Hospital in Washington D.C. Known as a lively-mannered woman who always seemed full of life, she had a continuing interest in civic work and local history and became interested in women's suffrage when in Washington D.C. [19]

It seems quite likely that Laura Porter was indeed an admirer of Susan B. Anthony, as well as of Elizabeth Wakeman Mitchell. Several photographs of Anthony belonging to Laura still exist in the collection of The Old Fort House Museum in Fort Edward, including one framed portrait on which is written on the back: *Susan B. Anthony, given at National Headquarters, Scotts Circle, in Senator Root's home, Washington D.C.* A December 11, 1915 issue of *The Suffragist*, a national suffrage magazine which belonged to one of the members of the Fort Edward Suffrage Club, describes a pageant about the life of Susan B. Anthony which was presented at Convention Hall in Washington D.C. on December 13, 1915. A list of characters revealed that Laura Porter was involved in this production as a member of the women's chorus. [20]

When she became active in local suffrage activities after returning to the area from Washington D.C., Laura worked with John P. Burke, a prominent man from Fort Edward. Locally, Mr. Burke was president of the International Brotherhood of Pulp, Sulphite, and Paper Mill Workers, and he was also the Chairman of the Industrial division of the Washington County branch of the New York State Woman Suffrage Party. The Glens Falls' *Post Star* described a meeting of the Fort Edward Suffrage Club at the home of Mr. and Mrs. Fred Davis on November 5, 1917 (the day before the statewide vote on female enfranchisement), where Burke urged: "I desire to call the attention of the Union men in this county who are voters to the fact that the AFL [American Federation of Labor], as well as the New York State Federation of Labor, has time and time again gone on record as being in favor of woman suffrage. All the prominent trade union leaders of the country, including Samuel Gompers, John Mitchell, and Frank Morrison, are heartily in favor of granting the right of suffrage to women of the state and nation. The 14th plank of the Economic Platform of the American Federation of Labor reads as follows: 'Woman suffrage co-equal with man suffrage.' I sincerely hope that the Union men of Washington County, at the coming election, will prove true to the highest ideals of the Labor Movement of this county by voting 'yes' on the woman suffrage amendment." [21]

John Burke was a very influential and well-respected man in Washington County, as was Men's League Chairman Erskine Rogers of Hudson Falls, and both men worked to encourage other men in the county to support female suffrage, aiding in its passage statewide in 1917. [22]

Encouragement and assistance to Laura Schafer Porter in her suffrage work also came from Gertrude Foster Brown – Mrs. Raymond Brown – Vice Chairman of the New York State Woman Suffrage Party, in this September 17, 1917 letter, just two months before the New York vote:

"My dear Mrs. Porter:

"We are very much pleased to learn from Mrs. Willis G. Mitchell of the organization of your club and want to welcome you warmly into the ranks of the New York State Woman Suffrage Party. We are the largest women's organization in the State and are affiliated with the National American Association, the great women's organization of the country, and we are all banded together for the most important cause in the world, that of freedom and equality for one-half of the human race.

"Those who are opposed to woman suffrage and some who believe in it are saying that the work for woman suffrage should be given up and that all the strength of the suffrage organization and the work of all its members should be given to the service of the country. That would be impossible. The suffrage bill is going to be voted on next November, war or no war, and we believe that the most patriotic service the women of New York State can give in this national crisis is to win the fight for democracy at the polls next November. This does not mean, however, that we are not exerting every effort in service to our nation—we are simply carrying the double burden.

"Our clubs everywhere are doing exceedingly effective work and are a source of much pride and interest to us. Our prospects are brighter than they ever were and the organization is progressing in leaps and bounds. Please convey to your club a warm welcome from the officers of the State Party, and I hope you will feel free to call on us at any time for any assistance we may give.

"Sincerely yours,
        Gertrude Foster Brown
        Vice Chairman – New York State Woman Suffrage Party" [23]

With friends and mentors like Elizabeth Wakeman Mitchell, Gertrude Foster Brown, John Burke, Erskine Rogers, and Susan B. Anthony, Laura Porter had the opportunity to learn the history of the struggle for the ballot while experiencing its activities from both Washington D.C. and Washington County, New York. Later in her life, she chronicled what she saw and experienced in both venues in an article that, it is believed, was never published, but which offered an articulate insight into one of rural upstate New York's noted suffragists. [24]   Reprinted in Fort Edward's Sesquecentennial publication in 1999, here is Laura in her own words:

"In the early 1900's and World War I, there was a feeling among women everywhere, a desire for more freedom and protection in their business interests and property rights, and a belief that there should be a law granting the opportunity to express a voice in selecting government officials and especially in town elections.   Schools needed women trustees as mothers wanted the best for the children's protection.   In these days, there was no P.T.A. [Parent-Teacher Association].

"A great thinker among women was Susan B. Anthony, who came before the public and spoke for Women's Rights in town halls, home gatherings, villages and cities all over New York State and finally nationally.   A few women leaders were Elizabeth Cady Stanton, Lucretia Mott, Dr. Anna Howard Shaw (a most marvelous woman), also a few others, and Dr. Mary Walker, a nurse who went on the battlefield to tend the sick and dying.   She wore men's clothes and could be seen anywhere in Washington D.C., with a black frock coat, gray striped pants, and a black silk formal hat.

"The writer [Laura Schafer Porter] met and spoke to her at the Capitol on her way to hear President Wilson talk on preparedness for World War I.   Her graying hair was cut rather short.   She was very quiet, firm and easy to talk with.

"Susan B. Anthony [was] ridiculed and punished many times but grew in stature just the same, and her influence spread throughout the state of New York, beginning from her modest home in Seneca Falls [actually Greenwich and later Rochester].   She was a great woman, admired for her fight for the rights of women and children.

"Later, Carrie Chapman Catt followed Dr. Anna Howard Shaw as the president of the newly established League of Women Voters [which had formerly been NAWSA]. Mrs. Catt, a very excellent speaker, a charming, fine looking, cultured woman, began going from town to town, state to state, and to England for votes for women.

"The newspapers were filled with ridicule at times, and the cartoonists enjoyed making fun of women asserting themselves.

"Carrie Nation, an English suffragist, was shown in the papers with a hatchet smashing windows in London, England. Carrie Nation was famous. She actually did go to saloons, smashed windows, and exposed vice.

"If a woman showed an inclination to voice her opinion, she was met with such remarks as, 'Oh! Now that's unladylike,' [or] 'Your place is in the home, in the kitchen,' [or] 'It's too rough for women to get out and mix with political parties, that's man's dirty work.'

"Mary Garrett Hay was another later suffragist from Ohio, a marvelous woman. Women were often cheated out of their property rights. The suffrage fever grew all over the country. And it came to Fort Edward through strong women who had to run a business or farm or owned land. Some were not married. Some men were interested and fought along with the women at home and in Congress.

"Erskine C. Rogers Sr., chairman of the men's committee, Hudson Falls, said 'It can be recorded that the men in Washington County declare their fairness to women, another proud fact in history.'

"In Canada and Russia, women were voting with men, making eight foreign countries which had women suffrage. Mrs. Erskine C. Rogers Sr., the former Annette Wakeman, and Betty Wakeman, were cousins of Susan B. Anthony.

"Mrs. Carrie Chapman Catt came to speak in all the towns and cities near us. She gave a wonderful talk at Bradley Opera House at which Mary Bradley was present because Mary and her mother had their many headaches over all the property Mr. Bradley owned, which was on the island, the Old Brown Row in Mechanic St., their handsome residence, a large brick house on McCrea St., and the Bradley Opera

House.

"Hudson Falls gave us Betty Wakeman Mitchell, who did a grand job, having a fine suffrage club there, and came to talk at Fort Edward. Fort Edward had many fine leaders who were suffragists from the early years. Among them were Mr. and Mrs. Fred Davis, Ida May Powell, Mr. and Mrs. Albert Wicks, Mrs. Sheridan Wait, Mrs. Thomas Lindsay, Miss Sarah Harris, Mrs. Matthew Redfern, Mrs. Laura Porter, Mary Bradley, and Mrs. Bradley, Mr. and Mrs. Harry Payne (Mr. Payne was the state engineer of the Barge Canal and Mrs. Payne was the first president of the Fort Edward Suffrage Club), John P. Burke was on the committee as industrial [chairman]. So John Burke and Mary Bradley were first to be on the board of Washington County to hold office in Fort Edward. Later, Sept. 12, 1917, a new president was chosen, Mrs. Laura Schafer Porter, and on that slate were the following: Leader – Mrs. Willis G. Mitchell of Hudson Falls; Vice Leader – Mrs. John Lake of Cambridge, Miss Mary Bradley of Fort Edward, and Miss Amelia Brasdell of Whitehall; Secretary – Mrs. Brodie G. Higley of Hudson Falls; Treasurer – Mrs. Preston Paris of Hudson Falls.

"Committees were: Church, Mrs. Thomas Bain of Argyle; Grange, Mrs. John MacDougall of Hudson Falls; industrial, John P. Burke of Fort Edward; men's, Erskine C. Rogers of Hudson Falls; press, Miss Nell Joan Dwyer of Hudson Falls; school, Miss Francis A. Tefft of Hudson Falls.

"Many humorous things were teased at the suffragists, such as 'Oh, you'll never get married,' [or] 'A woman's place is in the home,' [or] Don't butt in,' [or] 'Men want to run their own affairs,' [or] 'Politics is too rough for women!'

"Many meetings were held and one in particular was in the Baptist Church basement. Everyone was invited to attend and the writer was present. Here we discussed sending out mail and distributing dodgers all over Fort Edward, house to house. It took a great deal of courage to do it in the face of your own families and friends. Dodgers came from headquarters in New York City. Some were called 'Facts

Worth Knowing,' 'Votes for Women,' 'The Spirit of Democracy,' and many others which you must be sure to read on display soon in a Fort Edward store window, 'Oppenheim's.' One of our well-known men lost his nerve when his wife went from house to house to pass out suffrage notices. 'Oh! My, you must not pass that out,' he said.

"At that time we were trying to defeat Senator Wadsworth, who was running for reelection, as he was an anti-suffragist, and his wife was a radical against suffrage.

"The writer believed in suffrage before and after she was married and went to live in Washington D.C. She carried on her work for suffrage at the headquarters for 22 years all told.

"The headquarters was in the most beautiful exclusive Scotts Circle, the mansion of Elihu Root, U.S. Senator for many years. The writer's being president of the club in Fort Edward helped to give her a fine introduction, and she was made a hostess every Thursday afternoon to greet visitors and give information. All the National Board of Suffragists lived there. It was a great privilege to see daily the great women of America. There were 400 members in Washington.

"Our policy was not to be militant or official, or rough, and we were known finally as the League of Women Voters. There was another group in the city – a more militant group of whom we did not approve at all. The Woman's Suffrage Party later dissolved.

"Many congressmen's wives were active members as were educators, business women, scientists, professional actresses (drama and musical). Jane Addams – immortal now – famous of Hull House, Chicago, and ever so many leading American women came to us.

"Our first great job was to go to Congress to lobby and have interviews with senators and representatives, which we did in groups of three and four – never alone. The writer was used one time in the latter group; when we first went to lobby, there were four women: Mrs. Helen Gardener, the first woman commissioner of education; Mrs. Maud Wood Parks, national president of Woman's Suffrage;

Mrs. Yost, president of the Women's Christian Temperance Union; and the writer, formerly art teacher in a conservative Southern College, Due South, South Carolina. She was thus chosen to speak to the southern senators who were hard to convince, and was introduced as a believer and worker for suffrage.

"The suffragists gave many elaborate teas and receptions at their headquarters to honor celebrities, ambassadors and their wives. A huge reception was given for Jeanette Rankin of Wyoming, the first woman congressman. All the senators, judges, [and] representatives were invited. The writer was one of the many taking people to the reception line to meet Miss Rankin. The noted and colorful Speaker of the House of Representatives was Champ Clark, a southerner. It was a very hot evening. He was called upon for a speech. His face was florid. He wiped his head with a handkerchief, loosened his collar and said, 'There are more speeches given in Washington, and less listened to, than any other place in the United States,' at which everyone laughed and applauded.

"We gave a luncheon at the Carlton Hotel, honoring Lady Astor of England, a noted leader of the movement there. She was formerly a Virginian; also, later Madame Curie of France, the scientist who discovered radium, was entertained at the Woman's University Club.

"All cabinet officers during Wilson's administration were entertained by reception. Several hundred invitations were sent out monthly to these affairs. One particular occasion, they used this writer's handwriting for the invitations. President Wilson was for suffrage from the first [in the opinion of Laura Porter].

"An address-o-graph was used for hundreds of invitations by the writer, correspondence secretary. After five years of work, she was elected to the executive board for two years from 1930 – 1932. That was all done by her while holding a full time job an occupational therapist of the art shop at Walter Reed Hospital for 10 years.

"It was an experience and privilege to take part in a movement, freedom for women voters, during World War I, when history was made, and to be a pioneer in it in Washington, going to the Capitol for a few years to listen to speeches made by great men.  Washington was alive with men and women of note from all over the world.

"In 1919 came that great day [passage of the federal amendment granting suffrage to women; ratification came in 1920], that brought a thrill to every woman's heart in the League of Women Voters and crowds were at the Capitol, the House of Representatives, and the Senate.  The writer was present, and had a seat in the Gallery, along with all the other groups, senators, and representatives, and dignitaries.  It was a day to always be remembered.

"A spectacular sight was to see Senator Mann, a great worker and friend of suffrage, wheeled into the Senate in a wheelchair in order to be present. He had been ill and confined to a hospital.

"A joyous moment in history became a reality.  Susan B. Anthony's statue, in marble, is now in the rotunda of the Capitol, and a stamp was issued a few years ago in her memory.

"P.S. Susan B. Anthony taught school for the family of Lansing Taylor who lived on the corner of Route 4 and Moseskill [in Fort Edward]. She also taught and lived for a while in Greenwich."[25]


Noted Fort Edward suffragist Laura Schafer Porter died in 1966.

# Chapter VII
## Warren County Suffragists:
## Dr. Mary Putnam Jacobi and Mary Hillard Loines

As mentioned in Chapter 2, women's suffrage activities in Warren County, to the west of Washington County, varied – from the city of Glens Falls to the more rural, outlying areas, and along the shores of Lake George, in places like Bolton Landing where the monied classes of upstate and downstate New York and elsewhere spent their summers taking in the majestic beauty of the Adirondacks and the "Queen of American Lakes."

This chapter will focus on two distinguished suffragists from "downstate" who summered in Bolton Landing and who are claimed by Warren County in that regard: Mary Putnam Jacobi and Mary Hillard Loines. As women of educational achievement and wealth, they spoke out in favor of female enfranchisement. And, yet, their words and writings revealed that their basis for working for suffrage was not *class*-based but instead *gender*-based. Like Lucy Allen and Chloe Sisson, the two Marys pushed forward with the strength of their womanliness on behalf of the cause.

A closer look at Warren County first, however, reveals similarities and dichotomies in suffrage activity among the villages, towns, and the city of Glens Falls, and this provides an interesting backdrop for the stories of Mary Putnam Jacobi and Mary Hillard Loines.

Glens Falls, south of Lake George and Bolton Landing, from its 18th century founding was a city of lumber and saw mills and industries like limestone and cement. Its patriarchs were the powerhouses behind the building of railroads and canals, and the creation of electric power and world-class textiles. Its roots as a Quaker community, coupled with a populace open to arts, culture, and reformist ideas, made Glens Falls a ripe environment for debate on women's suffrage.

The New York State Woman Suffrage Party had an active Glens Falls branch, called the Glens Falls Political Equality Club, which was established in 1914 -- somewhat late, considering the earlier creation of PECs in Washington County.  The Glens Falls club sponsored lectures and debates on suffrage and worked hard on behalf of the cause throughout Warren County.  There is no doubt that the city dwellers were hungry for discourse on this topic, as evidenced by a plethora of newspaper articles in *The Post Star* in the first two decades of the 20th century, reaching a crescendo in 1914 – 1917.

On a frigid January night in 1915, a crowd of almost 1,000 gathered at Glens Falls City Hall to hear a lecture by Rabbi Stephen Wise, a proponent of the ballot for women.  In his address, he urged suffrage "as a matter of right and expediency," and because it is a right of people in a democracy. He proclaimed:  "Suffrage is a right and a prerogative in a monarchy, but is it *other* than a right in a democracy? Democracy means government by the people.  And, can you deny that women are included in 'the people?'" The crowd cheered. [1]

While Warren County's most populated community was open to the progressive idea of women voting, it also had its *anti* faction. A month after Rabbi Wise's speech, Alice Hill Chittenden, the President of the New York State Association Opposed to Woman Suffrage, drew an even larger crowd.  She expounded on her view that voting for women was unnatural and that the female vote would not lead to any positive impact on political corruption or to the amelioration of social conditions.  She argued:  "Democracy has nothing to do with the difference nature has imposed on the female and male.  Progress is based on natural laws and activities, and the two sexes are at a distinct variance. If you give the franchise to women, you double all the elements of the electorate. You will still have the dishonest voter." [2]

Anti-activist Chittenden had also spoken north of Glens Falls in the village of Lake George the previous summer.  On Saturday evening, July 11, 1914, she led an anti-suffrage meeting at the Court House.  In keeping with the pro and con format seen in the suffrage debates of Glens Falls, the pro-suffrage stance was given a month later in Lake George. On Wednesday evening, August 19, Mrs. Raymond Brown (the same Gertrude Foster Brown who had written to Laura Schafer Porter in Fort Edward) spoke at Union School on the topic: "Shall Women Be Given the Right to Vote?" Presiding over this public meeting was George Foster Peabody, president of the Men's League of the Warren County branch of the New York State Woman Suffrage Party.[3]

Peabody, a summer resident of Bolton Landing, marched in a suffrage parade in New York City in 1916 as a representative from Warren County.  He was a nationally known financier and philanthropist and was affiliated with the Spencer Track investment firm.  He was a man who was interested in the development of the United States during the late 19th century, and he became associated with many progressive projects and worthwhile endeavors. He was a good friend of Dr. Booker T. Washington, the president of Tuskegee Institute. He was asked by Woodrow Wilson to be the Secretary of the Treasury in his administration but did not accept.  Later on, he became one of Franklin Delano Roosevelt's *brain trusters* and was involved in the Tennessee Valley Authority.  Locally, he owned large tracts of land in the Lake George area.  In the late 1800's, he gave Prospect Mountain and Hearthstone Park to the State of New York.[4] Later in life, he married Katrina Trask (who will be the focus of Chapter 8), widow of his best friend, Spencer Trask, and they resided jointly in both Lake George and Saratoga Springs as they pursued their cultural, civic, and philanthropic ventures.

As a place defined in history and geography by the Adirondack Mountains, Warren County was characterized by some of the same features and contradictions that were found in the reform activities of the rural areas of Washington County.  A rugged way of life in the remote locations of Warren County engendered a spirit of male-female equality that led to pockets of pro-suffrage sentiment, much in the same way as the farming traditions of Washington County fostered a sense of gender equality which aided the cause.  The "underground railroad" was active in Warren County, and the temperance cause found solid moral footings among even the city residents southward in Glens Falls. In addition, the spirit of Susan B. Anthony was alive and active in the reformist movements of Warren County, as she hailed from nearby Battenville and Greenwich in Washington County and was a frequent visitor and lecturer in both these counties, and in neighboring Saratoga County.

An amusing anecdote exists about an incident with Susan B. Anthony at the Fort William Henry Motel in Lake George in 1856. Anthony, traveling on a suffrage speaking tour with one gentleman and two ladies, stopped for a luncheon at the luxury resort. During this period of strict social customs, it was acceptable only for men to dine at motels while traveling. Women were instead expected to remain in the carriage; it was customary for the men, upon returning from their dinner, to bring a cold provender to their wives or female companions who were awaiting them outside. However, when Susan's entourage arrived at the Fort William Henry, she and all of her group disembarked from the carriage and entered the dining room. The black waiter, who insisted only upon catering to the gentleman, became so flustered when Susan repeatedly recited from the menu those items she wished to order, that the manager had to be called. He eventually took Susan's order, as well as the orders of the other women, probably with a raised eyebrow, and all proceeded smoothly after that. [5]

The Lake George and Bolton Landing region of Warren County had become a popular tourist destination by the mid-to-late 1800's as rail and stagecoach routes extended into the Adirondacks. Travelers from Europe and America vacationed there, and a new wave of wealthy families built mansions along the road from Lake George to Bolton Landing on what came to be called "Millionaire's Row." Along with the influx of summer residents, many of whom were involved in industry, finance, medicine, and the arts, the local and indigenous population grew. Lumbering, mills, and tourism caused the Lake George – Bolton Landing – Warrensburg area to blossom by the turn of the 20th century. The mix of people and ideas that resulted created a fertile environment for the debate of some of the new century's most salient social issues, and women's suffrage was among those.

In 1893, as the 20th century neared, the following opinion (the author was a Bolton man) appeared in *The Warrensburg-Lake George News*:

"The women voting business is still very much to the fore. Our dear brothers are variously affected according to the degree of their development.

"One man insists that if his wife goes to the polls, she must have a quid of tobacco in her cheek, a pipe in her mouth, swear with the rest, and do and say other things not described. This illustrates his advancement in civilization, and his estimate of the value and sanctity of suffrage.

"Another worthy citizen declares his intention to 'boot' his wife, if she dares attempt to vote – whatever that means. Perhaps it means that he intends to always provide her with the loveliest shoes to be found. That is natural, of course. But perhaps it means something else, and very different.

"Women are so stupid about so many things it is hard to make them understand. Possibly they may learn in time, how to fold a ballot, and not swear over it.

"But, we still have one more type. He is the man who is afraid to have women vote for fear that they will to go war! Aren't you scared? We shall shiver – when it gets cold enough."[6]

*Mary Putnam Jacobi, circa 1880*

It is fascinating to think of how this expression of suffrage sarcasm and wit – or is it *anti*-suffrage in tone? – would have been viewed by Mary Putnam Jacobi as she read this piece in the local newspaper from her estate, Juniper Hill, overlooking Lake George. Mary had always been an avid advocate for women's rights and had lived her own life as a promotion of female social, educational, and political equality. The daughter of a publisher, she was born in 1842, grew up in New York City, and graduated from the New York College of Pharmacy in 1863. As a young woman in a man's profession, Mary was a pioneer. She served as a nurse in the Civil War and continued to be a trailblazer when she entered the Female Medical College of Philadelphia, and then went to work as a medical researcher at the New England Hospital. Setting her sights on becoming a doctor, she courageously applied and was accepted to the foremost medical school in the world at that time, L'École de Médicine in Paris – the first woman ever to do so. [7]

Throughout her life, Dr. Jacobi was an ardent spokesman for women's rights, suffrage, and socio-medical issues pertaining to women and children. She advanced ideas about women's biological systems to teach the medical community that women, biologically, are not the weaker sex. She was one of the first doctors in America to dispel the widely-held belief that women required rest during menstruation.

She became the president of the Association for the Advancement of Medical Education for Women and toured America and Europe in the late 1800's, lecturing about topics ranging from women's medicine to pathology to infantile paralysis. In the late 1890's, Mary Putnam Jacobi, along with Josephine Shaw Lowell, formed the Women's Municipal League in New York City. This organization focused on education about prostitution, women's social issues, and police corruption. [8]

Mary's husband, Dr. Abraham Jacobi, was a world-renowned pediatrician who was born in Prussia in 1830 and emigrated to

America in 1853 to flee the anti-Semitism that was spreading across Europe. [9] The doctors Jacobi came to Bolton Landing in 1867 and purchased Hiawatha Island in Huddle Bay, in Lake George. There they built their cottage, Juniper Hill, where they summered for many years as a retreat from their hectic lives as doctors and sought-after medical speakers. Sadly, they lost a young son, Ernst, at age eight; a stone monument in his memory still exists on the island. They later built a home adjacent to Juniper Hill for their daughter, Marjorie. [10]

The doctors devoted their lives to the betterment of women and children, enjoying their summers on Lake George until their later years. Both Mary and Abraham were supporters of women's suffrage and invigorated the larger debate about women's rights with their medical research and biological theories.

Mary earnestly spoke out in favor of suffrage – and did so from a biological and feminine point of origin. Believing in the inherent equality of the sexes, she became a formidable speaker on behalf of suffrage at a time when the debate was largely centered on democracy-driven arguments. As a doctor, a woman, and a mother, Mary was able to effectively articulate a new and fresh basis for political equality. And, as a pioneer for women's rights living at a time of American industrialization and the ensuing consequences of it for the roles of women in industry and changing definitions of womanhood, she boldly restructured the pro-suffrage agenda. [11]

Noted suffrage historian Ellen Carol DuBois commented on Mary Putnam Jacobi's particular contribution to the theoretical framework of the suffrage debate in the late 19th century, observing that she combined her upper-class perspective with the role she saw for herself as a woman. DuBois asserts that Jacobi used her *gender*, and not her *class*, on behalf of women's suffrage. [12]

Dr. Jacobi delivered an address on women's suffrage to the New York State Constitutional Convention in Albany in 1894. In that speech, she outlined her pro-suffrage stance as well as her views on the importance of the role of women as participants in modern American industrial society.    She later documented these ideas in a comprehensive pamphlet which has become a classic in suffrage literature, *Common Sense Applied to Woman Suffrage.*[13]

Among the papers of Easton suffragist Lucy Allen is an old newspaper clipping entitled, "Dr. Jacobi On the Woman Question." The content suggests that the article (from what newspaper Lucy obtained it is not known) is from about 1898. The heading states that this address was prepared by Mary Putnam Jacobi for a debate with a "Dr. Keene" of Philadelphia (who was evidently an anti-suffrage advocate), but which was never held.   Nonetheless, the eloquent writing by Mary in this piece underscored her unique blend of biological and philosophical beliefs in support of gender equality in modern society and her belief in the preciousness of womanhood in the political arena.   In her prepared remarks, she chronicled the history of humankind from ancient times to modern times and concluded that women's suffrage is a fundamental right.   In Dr. Jacobi's own words:

"I consider it a great honor to be allowed to meet Dr. Keene on this occasion, and to reply to the exposition of his views in regard to equal suffrage.   I hope he will not consider me disrespectful if I begin by saying that the various objections he has alleged seem to me to have really very little to do with the case -- about like the flowers which grow in the spring.   I would say the same thing of many of the arguments habitually urged in favor of equal suffrage.   The famous formula, 'Governments derive their just powers from the consent of the governed,' is inadequate.   It is not the consent but the advantage of the governed upon which the right to govern is based.   The form of government which confers the greatest amount of advantage upon those whom it professes to protect is the right form, the one which should be sustained, the one which should endure.   And, what is the greatest advantage?   Is it not evidently to obtain the largest amount of life possible -- to become the largest human beings?

"The most fundamental test between right and wrong which I can imagine is the test of the largeness of life.   For there is nothing more fundamental than force, and force tends incessantly to increase, to reproduce itself, to develop still further -- to grow.  This primary, irresistible tendency of all life, of all living things, to grow, is the deepest reason for the steady growth of democracy which has been going on from the times when all governments were summed up in the arbitrary decisions of the single tribal chiefs.

"People do not exist for the sake of providing orderly or dignified governments.  But governments exist for no other reason than to protect and favor and encourage and stimulate by every possible device the most vigorous thought and social activities of the mass of human beings over which they are set.  And it is a matter of observation that for the human mass no stimulant is so great as participation in the direction of public affairs.  When, at the end of the sixth century before Christ, the Athenian, Kleisthenes, overthrew the old aristocratic constitution of Solom, and brought all freemen into the deliberations of the State, so that every one voted except strangers, women, and slaves, an unparalleled degree of mental force was generated which sufficed to evolve the intellectual splendors of the age of Pericles, and also to sweep the Persians back across the Aegean Sea and save Europe from the domination of the Orient.  And from that moment, from the day of the battle of Marathon, for three centuries a splendid life animated those free Greek communities, a life which has been a beacon light for Europe for two thousand years, and only flickered and failed when the power of Rome intervened to take away the right of self-government and self-defence, in order to take better care of the citizens than they were supposed to be able to take of themselves, to silence their incessant political discussions, their active political life, and thus to prepare for the corrupt decadence of the Byzantine Empire.

"But all this mental power which has been so glorious was exactly coincident with the limits of the classes that exercised political responsibility, and from which women and slaves were excluded. They had no share in politics, no share in thought, no share in power, and only half a share in the evolution of European civilization -- and that is the way it has always been.  There is more inequality, more asymmetry, than in primitive savagery.  Society has limped like a girl with a curvature of the spine, one shoulder away up, the right shoulder belonging to the arm invigorated by the most strenuous work; the left shoulder feeble and drooping.

"At bottom, this whole question resolves itself into a biological problem; a theoretical question, to ascertain the true possibilities of human beings, and whether half of them are only half human; a practical problem, to find out how the weaker half can be brought up to the equal level that the unity of the social organism demands. It is this philosophical aspect of the case which chiefly attracts me. For I am far from believing that politics or political activities are the most interesting things in the world. I believe that the satisfaction experienced by Dr. Keene when the first patient recovered, from whom he had removed a tumor of the brain, was more than comparable with that with which at Canton, last November, Mr. McKinley received the announcement that he had been reelected President of the United States. But the triumphs of intellectual achievement are not for everybody; they are reserved for relatively few. The basic, elementary, social satisfactions and stimulations are those derived from the elementary social activities, that is, from politics; and in a vigorous social organism these should be distributed equally among all the members of that organization, therefore among women as well as among men. If there be any who do not want these, it is a proof all the more that they need them, and that society needs them to demand them.

"When women are ordered to confine themselves exclusively to personal and family life -- while men possess all that, and have political life in addition -- it is clear that women are reduced to exactly two-thirds of the life possible to men, hence are compelled to remain two-thirds smaller in general calibre. It is against this enforced reduction that women have begun to protest, just as so many other classes in the community have in succession protested, and in a successful of centuries have wrested for themselves political rights.

But I am wrong to say that women are only beginning to protest. Three thousand years ago, according to Virgil, when the Trojans, fleeing after the fall of Troy, travelled with their wives and children towards Italy in their uncomfortable row boats, they made a pause at Sicily to rest and celebrate the funeral games of Anchises.  From these, as from all major religious festivals -- the antecedents of our great political crises -- the women were excluded.  They withdrew in a body to the seashore, and to them, sitting clustered together, dull and depressed, Juno sent her messenger Iris, and stirred them up to utter their complaints.  With one voice they cried: 'Why, oh, why have we been dragged over this stormy sea, crowded together in the ships, enduring all the hardships together with the men, yet now are driven away from the splendid games that revive their energies?  True, the men alone sat on the benches and smote the waves with the oar; but, whenever the boat was landed, it was we who lit the fires, and dressed the food and cooked it, and dried the clothes of the men, saturated with the salt spray. Surely we have done our share; yet we are driven into this lonely corner!'

"Might we not imagine in the plaint embodied in Virgil's melodious lines an anticipation of the protest that might have been uttered by our New England foremothers, after their yet longer journey, and when they also had to bear the same hardships as the forefathers, and in addition to bear with the forefathers, yet never obtained equality in social or political rights?"[14]

What a strange historical coincidence that the words and ideas of world-renowned Dr. Mary Putnam Jacobi of New York City and Bolton Landing who died in 1906 found their way to Lucy Allen's farmhouse in Easton.  Tucked away in her papers, these paragraphs were no doubt taken to heart and used as eloquent inspiration by a Washington County woman who recognized a Warren County woman as her kindred spirit and respected mentor.

Not far from the Jacobi estate at Juniper Hill in Bolton Landing was Quarterdeck, the summer home of suffragist Mary Hillard Loines and her husband, Stephen.  Built in 1899, the estate (still extant today) also included a cottage, The Crow's Nest, and a home across the road, nicknamed Fo'cs'le. [15]

A contemporary of Mary Putnam Jacobi -- and also a downstate resident in the winter months and a "Millionaire's Row" resident in the summer months – Mary Hillard Loines shared with Jacobi a passion for social causes and reform. In a community activist career similar to Jacobi's, Loines was one of the founders of the Consumer's League in New York City and was active in prison reform.

Mary Hillard was born in England in 1844 into a shipping family. Her parents, John Hillard, originally of Boston, Massachusetts, and Harriet Low Hillard, of Salem, Massachusetts, brought young Mary at age three with them to settle in Brooklyn.  Even as a young woman, Mary was reformist-minded, and she dedicated herself to teaching former slaves after the Civil War.  Throughout her life, she was a supporter of the Tuskegee Institute. [16]

Along with her stance as an abolitionist, Mary Hillard Loines was active for over fifty years as a suffragist and on behalf of women's rights in New York State.  She was secretary of the Brooklyn Equal Rights Association (BERA); noted abolitionist Henry Ward Beecher was its vice president.  In 1869, she was a delegate from BERA to the first convention of the American Woman Suffrage Association. She went on to organize the Brooklyn Woman Suffrage Association, serving as its corresponding secretary for four years and as its president for nineteen years.  She was a member of the New York State Woman Suffrage Party's Legislative Committee for seven years, serving as its chairman from 1898 to 1904.  In 1899, she was one of a group of State suffrage party members to meet with newly-elected President Theodore Roosevelt to discuss women's suffrage. [17]

Mary Hillard Loines was a prominent figure in Brooklyn society, along with her husband, Stephen, who was a member of the maritime insurance firm, Johnson and Higgins.  Stephen died in 1919. The couple had three daughters, Hilda, Elma, and Sylvia – who followed in the footsteps of their mother as civic-minded feminists --  and a son, Russell, who died as a young man. [18]    Mary was a highly respected civic leader in Brooklyn and was chosen to write the Forward for *The Directory of Women in Civic, Economic, and Educational Affairs in Brooklyn To-Day, 1929 – 1930*; her photo appeared at the beginning of the pamphlet. In her Forward, she praised the "foresight and deep-thinking individuals" [19] who made Brooklyn what it was by that year and offered an eloquent overview of the features and institutions of that "mighty city." [20]

Also in this directory, Mary Hillard Loines penned a superb piece, entitled "When Suffrage Came to Brooklyn." Twelve years after New York State gave the franchise to women, and nine years after the ratification of the Nineteenth Amendment, she provided a history of the women's suffrage movement, starting from its antecedents as an emancipation movement sprung out of the Fifteenth Amendment. [21] She wrote about BERA and its reorganization in 1883 as the Brooklyn Woman Suffrage Association – the mission continuing to "promote the legal, industrial, and political rights of all American citizens, especially suffrage, without distinction of race or sex." [22] Mary concluded:

"In 1894, the Association secured thousands of names to the petition to the Constitutional Convention asking that the word 'male' be stricken out of Article II, Section I, of the New York State Constitution, which limited the ballot to male citizens. The Constitutional Convention having failed to adopt this amendment, a concurrent resolution providing for the change in the Constitution passed both houses of the Legislature in the spring of 1895. This was afterward declared void on a clerical technical error.

"For many years this Association was the only local suffrage organization in Brooklyn or New York, but in the early nineties [1890's] some of its members branched off, forming leagues in various parts of the city.

"The Brooklyn Woman Suffrage Association with entire faith in universal suffrage for men and women as the logical outcome of the democratic principles of the Constitution of the United States, was unceasing in its efforts to educate public opinion and hasten the day that at last in 1917, brought political equality to women.

"Then seeing that its work was accomplished, the Association voted to dissolve and celebrated the conclusion of its forty-ninth year, May 1917, by a luncheon at the Brooklyn Woman's Club, echoing the command of Huss [a 14th century Czechoslovakian religious thinker and reformer], five hundred years ago 'Lift up your head, oh! my daughter and recognize that you are a human being.'"[23]

Mary Hillard Loines complemented her Brooklyn suffrage activities with women's rights efforts in upstate New York during her summer sojourns in Bolton Landing. While there, she was a leading advocate of encouraging women taxpayers to participate in school district funding decisions, distributing circulars on this issue in Warren County in 1906. [24] She was an organizing member of the League of Women Voters in New York State as well. [25] Her name appears on the honor roll of suffrage leaders erected in 1931 at the New York State Capitol building in Albany by the League of Women Voters. [26]

Mary continued to spend her summers at Quarterdeck on Lake George until her later years. She died in Winter Park, Florida in 1944, at the age of ninety-nine.

*Mary Hillard Loines, circa 1940*

# Chapter VIII
## Saratoga County Suffragist:
## Katrina Trask

How political identity is formed in an individual – as seen in the lives and work of Lucy Allen, Chloe Sisson, Elizabeth Wakeman Mitchell, Laura Schafer Porter, Mary Putnam Jacobi, and Mary Hillard Loines – is a function of many contributors. Gender, heritage, environment, geography, religion, personal experience, mentorship, education, intellect, culture, and socio-economic status all probably play a role. The intersection of these factors with an historical moment in time helps political consciousness to percolate, and a foundation for belief springs forth.

In the pages of this book, the struggle for political equality by women of rural upstate New York at the turn of the 20th century has revealed the importance of innate womanliness in shaping their political identities and social perspectives. In embracing the strength of their places in their communities as women, wives, mothers, sisters, and daughters, they constructed a network of collaborators to facilitate the spread of their ideas and plans. They found inspiration in their women relatives and fellow reformers – town-to-town, county-to-county, within New York State, and across America – to motivate and build momentum for their suffrage cause. As suffrage leaders in their respective communities, each of these women demonstrated her understanding and conviction that uniquely feminine qualities are important ingredients for political reform. They read, they learned, they listened, and they helped and inspired one another. Taking full advantage of the growing freedoms for women as the new century was dawning, they harnessed their creative power as women citizens to demand full political equality. In the small towns and small cities of upstate New York, women's suffrage was a hot topic of the day, and regional women emerged as its spokesmen and leaders on both the local and national stage.

This chapter will focus on suffrage activity in Saratoga County, highlighting Katrina Trask – suffragist, writer, international peace activist, and patron of the arts.  A woman of great beauty, cultured intellect, and social conscience, Katrina epitomized the strength of womanliness in promoting reform.  Her style, grace, and elegance – not to mention her educated outlook on women's rights and world peace – made her beloved.  As a resident of both Saratoga Springs in Saratoga County (west of Washington County and south of Warren County) and Bolton Landing on Lake George in Warren County, she became a woman of great influence in upstate New York in the latter 19th and early 20th centuries.  Her biography is a favorite subject of regional history, and her legacy still today lives on vibrantly in the Saratoga and Lake George regions.

The history of the city of Saratoga Springs as a resort for the wealthy to bask in the healing mineral waters or visit the famous Saratoga Racetrack gave it a rich tradition as a popular place for health, tourism, recreation, and business.  In addition, its location in the northeast corridor of upstate made this community a crossover point for the "underground railroad" during the mid-19th century.  Slaves seeking freedom in Canada and those assisting them found routes northward from New York City and Albany that sent them straight into Saratoga County – and then veering eastward from Saratoga Springs into Washington County and northward to Canada; or, westward into the village of Ballston Spa or the towns of Milton or Corinth, and from there into Warren County and then north to Canada.  By 1827, slavery had been abolished in New York State – which had been among the largest slaveholding states prior to that. As a free state, then, by the mid-19th century, New York bred abolitionist sentiment, and, with advantageous geography as its destiny, became a place of refuge en route to freedom. Saratoga, Washington, and Warren counties, in particular, were a hotbed of anti-slavery activity and other reformist causes – most notably temperance and women's suffrage.

As discussed in Chapter 2, the interaction among the reformers of the antislavery, temperance, and suffrage movements in upstate New York was significant and engendered a sense of common purpose. While collaboration was, in fact, evident, there was still competition and rivalry, especially as each *cause* came into its own as a *movement* – needing to compete for leaders, financial resources, government endorsement, and the attention of the public.

Resort places like Saratoga Springs in the mid-to-late-19th century catered to a wealthy, cultured set who became a captive audience for reformist issues and who brought attention and influence to those causes in upstate New York and beyond. Well-known reformers like abolitionists Frederick Douglass, Abel Brown, Gerrit Smith, and William Lloyd Garrison; suffrage leaders Susan B. Anthony, Matilda Jocelyn Gage, Mary Anthony, Lucy Stone; and temperance leaders William Hay all traveled and lectured in the Saratoga Springs vicinity. The entire Saratoga, Warren, and Washington counties region, with its Quaker and Baptist communities and homegrown reform leaders, made it conducive to the spread of progressive ideas, including women's suffrage.

Suffrage historian Doris Weatherford described the brilliant savvy of Susan B. Anthony in choosing Saratoga Springs as the venue for her suffrage work in the mid-1850's. Recognizing its allure as a playground for the wealthy and for Southerners seeking the cool mountains and lakes of the Adirondack region during the oppressive summer heat, Susan organized rallies and lectures in the resort city. As early as 1854, she, along with suffragist Matilda Jocelyn Gage (with whom she and Elizabeth Cady Stanton would later collaborate on the writing of the multi-volume set, *The History of the Woman Suffrage Movement*), spent summers there speaking and raising money for suffrage and working to influence public opinion on behalf of the cause. In 1855, Anthony sold 20,000 pamphlets about women's rights in Saratoga Springs. For the next decade, women's rights advocates flocked to the city to fundraise and speak for suffrage to the rich and powerful patrons gathered there. [1]

On August 15, 1855, *The Daily Saratogian* reported that Susan B. Anthony called to order the New York State Women's Rights Convention in the former St. Nicholas Hall on Broadway.[2] Reverend (and well-known suffragist) Antoinette Brown declared several resolutions; among them was: "It is high time to inaugurate a new era in civil and political government, to resurvey the rights and reconstruct the duties and privileges of men, and to recur to first principles and hold fast to the nature and inalienable rights of our race as life, liberty, and the pursuit of happiness. We cordially rejoice to know that these principles are more and more consistently applied to the male citizens of New York State; and we only demand that they should be as consistently extended to females also. For this reason we claim for women the right of suffrage, fully, freely, and universally."[3]

Also present at this two-day convention was nationally-renowned suffragist, Lucy Stone, who was married to noted abolitionist Henry Blackwell. As one of the original leaders of the national suffrage movement along with Anthony, Stanton, and Mott, Lucy Stone was a much-admired speaker. In Saratoga Springs, she spoke out on behalf of suffrage and also alleged that the lack of education and equality for women led to deleterious societal consequences: "The great cause why women become vicious – why unhappy marriages are contracted – why children are neglected, and not brought up as they should be, is owing to defective education, to the limited number of employments to which society and custom have opened to women, and to their ill-paid toil."[4] Suffrage rhetoric even in 1855 was beginning to connect the winning of the franchise to the general elevation of women's status in society as wives, mothers, workers, and educated citizens.

Most likely present at this suffrage meeting in Saratoga Springs in 1855 was Sarah Anthony Burtis, a second cousin to Susan and Mary Anthony. Born in 1810 in the town of Saratoga, she married Louis Burtis, a Quaker, who was originally from Troy, New York.[5] Sarah Burtis was a pioneer in retail business in the city, becoming the first woman ever in Saratoga Springs to hold a salesclerk position, which she obtained in the store of a Mr. White.[6] She was an ardent worker for suffrage, as well as for antislavery, entertaining leaders of the abolitionist movement – Frederick Douglass, William Lloyd Garrison, and Wendell Phillips – at her home on Spring Street, which was believed to be a stop on the "underground railroad". Sarah was also an avowed *ultraist* – who was a person adhering to Spiritualism, as well as to women's rights and abolition.[7]

The flourishing of women's rights sentiment in Saratoga Springs and Saratoga County continued into the later decades of the 1800's. An elegant doyenne of a stately Georgian manor built on the outskirts of the city in 1893 -- Katrina Trask -- would become a suffragist of great influence in upstate New York and the United States. And, it would be she, along with other prominent women's rights advocates, who would come to redefine the women's movement when the vote was won. A woman of exceptional beauty, intellect, and understanding of the power of femininity in society, Katrina participated in ushering in a new era of feminist reform and womanly influence and became known the world over for her writings advocating international peace during World War I. From her estate, Yaddo, in Saratoga Springs, and from her summer home, Triuna, on Three Brothers Island in Lake George, she was a respected voice in the women's rights and suffrage movement in turn-of-the-20th-century upstate New York.

Born Kate Nichols in Brooklyn, New York in 1853 to Dutch and English parents, Katrina married wealthy New England financier Spencer Trask in 1874. They purchased property in Saratoga Springs from Revolutionary War veteran Jacob Barhyte, building a magnificent estate, later named Yaddo by their four-year daughter Christina, in 1893. Ever creative, with a flair for dramatic artistry and culture, Katrina made the Trask home a spectacular residence – complete with elegantly furnished rooms and staircases, exquisite gardens and fountains, and exciting holiday parties and pageants.

Despite their charmed life, however, the Trasks suffered great tragedy: their four children all died at very young ages. Daughters

Christina and Katrina and son Spencer Jr. all died within days of each other after contracting diphtheria from their mother. Another son, Alan, drowned in a small lake on the Yaddo property.

Grief-stricken over the deaths of her beloved children, Katrina turned to writing. She wrote novels, short stories, plays, poems, and essays – mostly on historical and literary themes – often publishing them without using her true name – as she struggled to reclaim her balance and happiness in life. [8]

Tragedy struck Katrina Trask again in 1909 when her husband was killed in a gruesome railroad accident. Spencer Trask was a successful businessman who had been instrumental in securing contracts for early street lighting in American cities, and he was a large stockholder in *The New York Times*. He was a great philanthropist and friend to Saratoga Springs, saving the mineral springs from depletion by carbonic gas manufacturers. In addition, he persuaded his friend from Glens Falls, New York Governor Charles Evans Hughes, to purchase lands for what is now Saratoga Spa State Park.[9] Hit hard by the Panic of 1907, Mr. Trask was still trying to recover financially at the time of his death.

Alone at Yaddo, Katrina continued her writing, as well as her involvement in social and philanthropic causes. During this time, she authored perhaps her best-known work, *In the Vanguard*, an anti-war play that revealed her belief in Christian teachings as the foundation for world peace. Other writings by her included the play, *Without the Walls*, and essays, *The Virgin Birth*, *The Obligation of the Inactive*, and *Motherhood and Citizenship: Women's Wisest Policy.* [10]

Mrs. Trask's commitment to the arts and culture led to her desire to create a haven for serious creative professionals. She turned her own estate into a retreat for writers, artists, musicians, and composers where they could live and work in splendid, bucolic, and quiet surroundings. Yaddo, the artists' retreat, was officially opened in 1926 and is still operating today. [11]

Prior to creating this retreat for artists, Katrina, along with Spencer (before his death) and family friend, George Foster Peabody, established a vacation retreat for the young working women of the shirt and collar textile mills in the city of Troy, near Albany. She had become aware of the social conditions, low pay, and long hours of the factory girls through humanitarian Mary Wiltsie Fuller, whose father was a partner in the Fuller and Warren Stove Company in Troy. Mary Fuller had established the Girls' Friendly Society, an Episcopalian organization which gave young working women a chance to enjoy low-cost vacations. In 1902, Spencer, Katrina, and George partnered together and commissioned renowned New York City architect Stanford White to design and build a Lake George vacation spot. The result was *Wiawaka* – the resort being given an Indian name meaning "the eternal spirit in women."[12]  Rates were $6 per week or $1 per day, and 50 cents per meal – about half the cost of other Lake George hotels and motels. Swimming, boating, fresh pine air, walking, and relaxing were now to be within the affordable reach of the hardworking factory girls.[13]

The concerns of women, mothers, and young working women in northeastern New York's industries were ever-present in Katrina Trask's mind. They were revealed in her writings and were also the beneficiaries of her fortune. As a proponent of women's rights and suffrage, she began to direct her writing talents toward this end.

On October 13, 1917 – a month before New York State male voters went to the polls to rule on women's suffrage – Katrina was the featured author in *The Woman Citizen*, a publication of *The Woman's Journal*, which had been founded in 1870 and was the official

*Katrina Trask, circa 1917*

newspaper of the National American Woman Suffrage Association (NAWSA). [14]   In this comprehensive article, entitled "Woman Suffrage a Practical Necessity," Katrina declared herself to be devoted to the cause of female enfranchisement and defended herself against detractors who had branded her an "anti." With a stunning picture of her accompanying the article, she traced the evolution of her thoughts on the issue of suffrage and beautifully articulated the unique aspects of womanhood which, she asserted, made women equal to men as citizens. [15] In so doing, she expertly proclaimed that "woman's supreme mission" is womanhood and exalted that this and motherhood are the ultimate power of womanly potential in the world.[16] Her argument was masterful, and her basis for reasoning seemed beautifully akin to the suffrage writings of her Washington County neighbor, Lucy Allen of Easton.

Here is Katrina's essay:

"In these fateful days, women are serving the country in valiant and amazing ways:   they are developing new faculties and they are performing strenuous, undreamed-of and almost impossible tasks.

"I am convinced that to help them in the performance of these tasks it has become necessary for them to have the Franchise.

"Therefore, I have enrolled my name as a member of the Woman Suffrage Party and hope that I may be permitted to render that Party some slight service.

"I rejoice to be associated with the splendid women who form the Party and who so unselfishly serve it.

"I am constantly and earnestly asked what has led to my conversion.

"If my 'conversion,' as it is called, means a converting of my energies and my endeavors into work for the Party, which I have hitherto steadfastly refused to join, then the expression is correct.

"If by conversion is meant the turning away from or the change of my ideal and theory on the subject, then it is incorrect; there has been no change whatsoever. I still hold my old opinions and my theory about woman and woman's mission. But I have changed my *course* to meet the perilous times.

"I do not think that my position is of interest to the readers of *The Woman Citizen*, but as the editor of that able paper has courteously urged me to state my position I will do so.

"Before I state what my position is, I should like to state explicitly what my position has NEVER been. I never was – I never could have been- an anti-suffragist. In a progressive age, where evolution is the law of life, I should think that anyone would hesitate to be *anti* to any movement for any cause (not involving a moral issue) that a large body of earnest, conscientious persons were striving to accomplish.

"I did not refuse to join the Party because of the disagreeable and undignified methods incident to the movement, although they greatly repelled me and offended my taste – such for example as the militant outbreak in England and the picketing in the United States.

" I well knew that there never has been any great movement, any organization or party without its crass and deplorable attendant evils which do not affect the fundamental truth and purpose of the organization.

"It would be quite absurd to keep out of the Democratic Party because there is a Tammany or to keep out of the Republican Party because there is a Philadelphia Ring. Moreover, I knew that the National American Woman Suffrage Association denounces this objectionable conduct and concentrates its efforts on securing, in a dignified way, what it considers a legitimate political end.

"As I was not opposed to suffrage in itself; as I was not deterred by the violent methods associated with the movement, and as the Party was working for precisely the very thing I most ardently desired, namely, the emancipation of woman – why then did I refuse to join the Party? For this reason:

"I differed radically from the Party as to the relative value of the ways of approach and of procedure in securing the highest emancipation for women.

"The Woman Suffrage Party believes that the spiritual emancipation of women can be developed better and more truly after it has gained political freedom.

"I strongly felt that political freedom would be a danger, rather than a good, until women had first gained their needed spiritual emancipation and had become possessed of the winged freedom of their own souls.

"I felt that the Party was sacrificing the greater for the less, and that, in focusing its attention on the political end, it was reversing the highest order, and thereby postponing the highest accomplishment.

"This does not mean that I objected to the vote, not at all. Although personally I never desired it, I had no objection whatever to women having the vote.

"Whether or not they had it seemed to me an unimportant matter – as compared with other things. I saw no reason why a woman should not cast her ballot precisely as she paid her taxes, neither emphasizing nor protesting against the one nor the other.

"I recognize the full value of the franchise. I am a democrat, and, of course, the democratic plea appeals to me – the plea that women are of the people and there cannot be a complete democracy until all the people vote.

"This is true; but I felt that there was a greater good for women which should be considered first. I wanted women to work for a great spiritual good, a spiritual awakening to their possibilities; this in no way interfered with the final having of the franchise; but it postponed it.

"In the meantime, they could afford to wait; they were not without vast power in the present case. I was distressed that the wise body of intelligent women in the Party did not admit this – did not urge it.

"The essence and true value of the franchise has always lain in women's hands – if they knew how to obtain it – whether or not they had the actual political advantage of the ballot. All that can be gained by them in having the practical privilege of the vote was theirs in reality, if they but knew how to grasp their opportunity and had cultivated their power to possess it.

"I feared that, in the hectic feverish work for the letter of the law, women might lose 'the spirit, which maketh alive,' or, at any rate, they were postponing its quickening.  It was as though I saw thirsty women, hustling and bustling, toiling and moiling to dig a cistern when all that was necessary was for them to clear away the camouflage covering the crystal spring of water welling at their feet – clean, pure and living.

"I keenly regretted to see such noble women, as the leaders of the Woman Suffrage Party, throwing their genius and their wonderful energy into what seemed to me to be of minor importance, while they allowed the great essential to wait.

"I hesitate to say anything that even suggests a criticism of those whom I so much admire and who have practically laid down their lives for a cause; but I must make quite clear what prevented me from sooner giving them my cooperation.

"I felt we could work for the vote, if need be, *after* we had given our attention and our zeal to the study, the contemplation, the exaltation of woman's supreme mission – Womanhood!

"I felt so strongly that the crying need of the world was an emancipation of the latent quality in woman that I was impatient to have the intellectual effort and phenomenal energy of my spirit-sisters diverted from the great channel of opportunity.

"By womanhood, I do not mean anything so limited as the mere sex differentiation which our grandmothers taught should control women's lives.  The stock argument of those opposed to woman suffrage is tiresomely obvious, viz:  that woman's place is in the home. Of course it is! I understand that the intelligent women of the Woman Suffrage Party not only admit this, but urge it. The question, however, is not – Where is woman's place? The question is – What should she do with that place? She should learn to make her place a larger place – her home a loftier home. It lies with woman to make the home more stimulating, more vivid, more heroic, and not allow the home to make her more petty, more dull, more insignificant.

"Woman should magnify the home into a Palladium and not be dwarfed by the home into a Drudge.

"This is woman's true emancipation. It was this I wanted women to ponder, that when the vote came to them they would be more evolved to use it.

"I felt that the time, the feverish energy, spent on securing the vote diverted women's attention from the great Endeavor with which they should concern themselves.

"Woman have never grasped (except in individual cases) the *noblesse oblige* of their high calling; to do so I felt was their paramount duty: the first thing to be studied, to be investigated, to be contemplated, to be sought.

"Women have been endowed with a distinct and different quality from men; to them has been given a latent power, a divine force which has never been estimated, cultivated nor admitted. They, themselves, have never even claimed it; they are not really conscious of it. It is the quality which sets them apart in the great creative scheme – it is a sublime potentiality of which Motherhood is the glorious expression, the luminous crown.

"Nor do I mean by Motherhood anything so limited or so material as the mere physical bearing of children, although even this physical function holds an opportunity for women with which there is nothing comparable in the realm of Nature.

"Every human being in the world has been born of woman, has lain, for months, under her heart in the holiest bond that God and Nature have ordained; then the child has been given into her arms and left like wax in her hands during the formative and impressionable years.

"There is no limit to what she might accomplish were she really awake and faithful; she might sow seeds that would bear fruit in a harvest of inestimable good for her own reaping.

"It is an unspeakable opportunity; a supreme right, far beyond the right that any vote could give.

"But I mean something larger than this. I mean spiritual Motherhood – a universal thing – the great expression of the power latent in woman, her birthright, greater than any political right, which, were it developed, would fit her for any place, for any sphere.

"This is hers whether or not she has borne children; it endows her with a divine possibility.

"In fact, I sometimes think that the highest type of Motherhood has been achieved by those women from whom the completion of love has been withheld and who have grown heroic through the noble bearing of their sacrificial sorrow.

"It is this special spiritual talent, this psychological endowment given to woman by the Creator, which, I felt, should be studied to become in every phase of life an operative force.  It is a power which, if rightly cultivated and developed, might transform the world.

"Scoffers may doubt it – that does not disprove its existence; scoffers doubted for centuries the great electric forces that lay unrecognized and unharnessed in the world; scoffers doubted for years the psychological laws, and those laws are now factors in all branches of life – even in the practical science of therapeutics.

"Woman herself may question this divine potentiality, may doubt this dynamic power hidden in the depths of her strangely coordinated, complex nature.

"I never doubted it; I never questioned it; I believed always in this God-given mission of woman and that it was her first, supreme obligation to emancipate this latent force.   I was impatient that, instead of working for the vote, the genius of the Party did not concern itself with organizing some great movement to work for the emancipation of this dynamic power, educating women how to possess it, to cultivate it, to develop it and to proclaim it.

"It was an ideal, perhaps, but it seemed to me, also a practical working basis for betterment.

"Now, however, the whole aspect of life has changed; the whole world, for three-and-a-half years, has been in a mad upheaval [World War I].  One's theories and one's ideals must wait for fulfillment upon the issue of this tragic crisis.  Meanwhile we must adapt ourselves to the crisis and seek all practical helps to meet it.

"To walk calmly on, hugging one's dear ideals, no matter how dear those ideals my be, when the ground is rocking and trembling from a violent earthquake, shows a petty mind, and it is the petty mind alone which, as Emerson points out, fears inconsistency.

"All those who have been kept out of the Party, as I have been, because they desired to work for a larger emancipation for woman than the vote could bring; all those who worked against equal suffrage because they honestly held the potent objection that it would make more political confusion; all those who shrank, with natural reluctance, from the added responsibility the ballot would entail, should now join the Party, because it is necessary for the women, who are bearing the burden of the day.

"All the men who feared they knew not what if the vote were granted to women and who have justly been repelled by the militant manifestation which, to their credit, contradicts their highest ideal of woman, should see that, now, equal suffrage is a needed measure, and they should be quick to grant it.

"Extraordinary and utterly unforseen conditions beset women:  most unexpected responsibilities and unprecedented duties have been thrust upon them, and they must have an immediate equipment to meet these demands.

"The vote is practical equipment. The vote will help women in their work; it is a national asset, valuable in this emergency.

"Men are going to the war: they will return, God help them, disabled and impaired. Women must loyally take the active work, the vital responsibility for the common good; and as suffrage gives to so many of them strength for this task, they ought to have it.

"Women have been called upon to share in every possible preparation, in every national endeavor, and they have answered with a quick and eager affirmative.

"As the franchise gives them a sense of surety and security, a feeling of co-operation with the Government which they are so quick to serve, it should not be denied them.

"Women are willing to stand beside men in the lurid waste of the present holocaust, working and planning in ways that stagger men's belief – sacrificing, enduring, smiling, strengthening and sustaining; and, as the franchise would sustain and give added strength to at least one million New York women (by actual poll), New York men should be quick to grant it, from the sense of justice of which they boast and by their latent chivalry.

"Yaddo, Saratoga Springs, New York – October 2, 1917."[17]

Coincident with Katrina Trask's piece in *The Woman Citizen*, her longtime friend George Foster Peabody likewise was supporting the cause, writing and speaking on its behalf in Saratoga and Warren counties and serving as chairman of the Men's League of the Warren County Chapter of the New York State Woman Suffrage Party. Writing from Saratoga Springs on February 13, 1917, eight months prior to Katrina's article, Peabody composed this Letter to the Editor of *The Post Star* in the neighboring city of Glens Falls:

"This is, beyond question, the great crisis of the history of humanity in this world as we approach the ending of the war and the settlement of the issues. It seems clear that the neutral nations, if dominated by a high and unselfish realisation of the universal brotherhood of man will be called on to have a large part in shaping the rebuilding of civilization during the remainder of the century.

"It is vital, therefore, that the United States of America, and especially New York, its greatest state, shall mobilize all the resources of heart and mind and conscience to do the wisest thing in the best way with wholeheartedness.

"No permanent advice of mankind is ever made without woman's cooperation, and in the great evolution of moral force more fully applied in government, the thing most needed is that women shall be conscious of their equal responsibility with men.   Nothing ever develops character and calls forth true wisdom as does responsibility. It is of the utmost consequence, therefore, that this year 1917 shall signalize the advance of New York State by granting women their inherent right to say their full conviction as to government by having equal voting rights with the men.

"I think this is by far the most important question of the time or any time in the future and believe men as well as women should now consecrate their best endeavors in the campaign of 1917 for suffrage for women in New York State." [18]

Like Katrina Trask, George Foster Peabody had intellectualized the natural rights of women as voting citizens and had the prescience to know that women's participation in politics and world affairs could have a positive effect on humankind, civilization, and world peace.

As kindred spirits and lifelong friends, Katrina and George eventually married, in 1921, living at Yaddo where Katrina had been confined for several years as a semi-invalid.  She died in 1922, leaving behind a legacy of cultural advancement, social reform, women's rights and suffrage, and womanly influence for peace and equality. George went on to serve President Franklin Delano Roosevelt and died in 1938. His ashes were buried with Katrina's in the Rose Garden at Yaddo. [19]

# Chapter IX

## Success for Suffrage:
## Womanly Influence and Citizenship

*"The right of citizens of the United States to vote shall
not be denied or abridged by the United States or by
any state on account of sex. Congress shall have power
to enforce this article by appropriate legislation."*

*-Amendment XIX of the United States Constitution
(ratified August 26, 1920)*

T he culmination of suffrage activity in Washington, Warren, and Saratoga counties came on November 6, 1917 when New York State granted women the right to vote. This was a major step toward progress in the passage of a federal amendment, since the New York victory gave the needed votes in the House of Representatives toward its adoption. Equal suffrage was eventually proposed by Congress on June 14, 1919 and ratified on August 26, 1920, becoming the nation's Nineteenth Amendment.

Newspapers in the upstate New York region on November 7, 1917 were jubilant with the news of the state suffrage victory. And, for the first time, suffrage articles made their appearance on the front pages. News stories describing activity at the polls, and where and how local suffragists worked and campaigned for the cause, were seen in print, as were comprehensive pieces which included voting results, by election districts, in upstate counties.[1]

In the statewide vote, suffrage was carried by approximately 80,000, according to *The Post Star* in Glens Falls. In Warren County, however, it was dealt a blow – being defeated by only nineteen votes. The city of Glens Falls, though, supported women's suffrage with a win by 179. An article from *The Post Star* on November 8 described the typical local reaction to the passage of women's suffrage: "A reporter from *The Post Star* talked to many women who were not suffragists and all said they would probably vote. Men who were openly against suffrage said yesterday that as long as the decision for suffrage had been reached that they would try and induce the women members of their family to vote. One man said: 'As long as some of the women are going to vote, why not try and have them all do so. If they all vote, suffrage will be a success. If some fail to vote, it will be a failure.'"[2]

Saratoga County supported female enfranchisement by over 1,000 votes.[3]

In Washington County, suffrage was carried by a majority of 188. The Hudson Falls Political Equality Club and Betty Wakeman Mitchell must have rejoiced to hear the results – the vote was carried by 218 in Hudson Falls. In Fort Edward, however, it lost by five, surely a sad day for Laura Schafer Porter and her PEC. The town of Easton supported suffrage (by eighteen votes), causing happiness in its PEC and with its leaders, Lucy Allen and Chloe Sisson.[4]

Women's suffrage had been defeated in New York in November 1915 by 190,000, with 1.2 million men voting. Two years later, however, female suffrage passed, making New York the last state to grant women the right to vote before the passage of the federal amendment in 1920.

NAWSA President Carrie Chapman Catt's "Winning Plan" – to focus the suffrage fight on pushing for federal approval instead of battling state-by-state – was a brilliant tactical maneuver, and, along with the building of powerful, inclusive coalitions among suffrage organizations, women of all socio-economic classes, black and immigrant women, and working women, victory was finally achieved.

The untold story of suffrage success, however, lies in the role played by local suffragists and suffrage groups who became the engines for political change at the grassroots level. Inspired by the national movement and its leaders, women like Lucy Allen, Chloe Sisson, Elizabeth Wakeman Mitchell, Laura Schafer Porter, Mary Putnam Jacobi, Mary Hillard Loines, and Katrina Trask went to work in the small communities of northern upstate New York to push for political equality.   Finding strength from their places as women in the rural areas and small cities of the tri-county area, each of these women forged alliances and partnerships with other women and reformers in order to press for equality in citizenship.  Peacefully and powerfully, the suffragists profiled in this book advocated for equal footing with men in the political arena.  They used their First Amendment rights and the familiar places and institutions of their communities to create their own political arenas from which to boldly act and express themselves on the subject of suffrage.  They utilized the broad planks of their own political identities as citizens to articulate the reasons why women must be included among the voting electorate, and they did it with intelligence, grace, and savvy – never failing to call upon their gender specific characteristics as women, wives, and mothers to support their arguments.

In a very real way, the rhetoric and writings of Lucy, Chloe, Betty, Laura, the two Marys, and Katrina stand apart from much of what was expressed on the national suffrage scene, for their words, attitudes, and actions show an emphasis on femininity for the cause that was not typically seen from pro-suffrage advocates.  In fact, their focus on womanliness was a tactic often seen in the work of *anti*-suffragists.  This uncommon, and seemingly contradictory, aspect of the work of the ladies profiled in this book makes them deserving of our attention, study, and respect.  Shaped by the essence of their psyches as women, they blended the influences of their geography, family, friendships, mentors, religion, political consciousness, and sense of civic duty to energize and invite a commitment for reform.  Strength of purpose was matched by their conviction *not* to compromise their true natures as women in the world.  In their ordinariness they were extraordinary, and it is fitting that their places in history now be unveiled.

Whether measured by the activity of the rural Easton PEC, or the activities of the suffrage clubs in the small villages of Hudson Falls and Fort Edward, or in the small cities of Glens Falls and Saratoga Springs, northern upstate New York was a pivotal stage in the women's suffrage movement in the late 19th and early 20th centuries. And, whether they were lesser-known suffragists like Lucy Allen and Chloe Sisson, or more well-recognized suffragists like Mary Putnam Jacobi and Mary Hillard Loines, each of these remarkable women played a powerful role in the achievement of female enfranchisement in New York State in 1917. As people whose lives straddled two centuries, they were truly the first women of the modern era.

The 20th century brought industrialization, war, globalization, and a transformation in the roles of women in society. Women gained new freedoms and opportunities – at the ballot box, in education, in the workplace, in the home -- and in the bedroom. Relations between the sexes found new measures of equality -- and new areas of conflict – as the century progressed. Politically, women asserted themselves slowly, yet steadily, as the decades rolled on. Twenty-six million women voted in the Presidential election of 1920, electing Warren Harding as the United States' 29th President.

After 1920, the National American Woman Suffrage Association transformed itself into an instrument of civic education for new women voters, becoming the League of Women Voters, which remains very active today, and counts both men and women in its membership.   Many suffrage leaders, like NAWSA's Carrie Chapman Catt and Saratoga Springs' Katrina Trask, became spokeswomen for international peace efforts as the world recovered from the ravages of World War I.

The lesson of suffrage success on the local, regional, and national levels is that inclusion and commonality of purpose can bring about positive change. Being true to one's gender identity, racial and/or ethnic heritage, religion, family, and accounting for the affect of one's geographical surroundings can and does foster understanding and the betterment of society. The women, famous and not-so-famous, who participated in the fight for the right to vote in New York State and

America understood this magical mixture and capitalized on it to win. And, from the farms of Washington County, to the shores of Lake George, and to the opulent halls of Yaddo, the suffragists of upstate New York captured the attention of their region as they parlayed their womanly influence to success.

Perhaps there will never be room enough in history books for the stories of the unknown people who fought for the rights of women in the centuries gone by – and who still fight on today – but let this book be a start. And, let no woman say that she cannot achieve or influence because she is denied rights or opportunities because of being female. Instead, let the stories of Lucy, Chloe, Betty, Laura, Mary, Mary, and Katrina help us to see what extraordinary human progress can occur when the moral compasses of women stay centered on their womanliness-- and that all women can achieve and influence *because of it.*

# Chapter X

## "Honor the Ladies:"
## The Legacy of the Easton Political Equality Club

On Saturday, October 2, 2004, a program called "Honor the Ladies" was held in Easton, New York at Burton Hall, on Route 40, in the north end of town. This evening of storytelling and music was presented by the Trustees of the library in honor of the amazing Easton Political Equality Club (PEC), the first of its kind in rural northeastern New York and a powerful force in Washington County and state suffrage work. [1]

Well-known regional storytellers Nancy Marie Payne and Kate Dudding presented dramatic renderings of the lives and work of Easton suffragists, Lucy Allen and Chloe Sisson as they blazed new trails for women's political and voting rights. [2]

*"Honor The Ladies"*
*Booklet Cover, October 2, 2004*

The exquisite musical talents of L'Ensemble, a quartet made up of musicians from New England were also featured at the event. Ida Faiella, a soprano vocalist, was joined by pianist Charles

Abromovic, violinist Barry Finclair, and cellist Semyon Fridman in presenting the musical compositions of three women composers – Maria Theresia Von Paradis (1759 - 1824), Amy Cheney Beach (1867 – 1944), and Clara Wieck Schumann (1819 – 1896) – who were historical heroines with the same commitment to female equality as the ladies of the Easton PEC.[3]

"Honor the Ladies," sponsored in part by public funds from the New York Council on the Arts Decentralization Program and the Lower Adirondack Regional Arts Council[4], was a huge success, and, for the first time, brought to life the extraordinary story of the Easton PEC and its two leading suffragists.

Like this significant historical tribute to the ladies of Easton held in the fall of 2004, this book serves to uncover and tell the story of these remarkable women and their bold actions to win voting rights for women. Perhaps for the first time, the work of the small Easton PEC in rural Washington County in northeastern New York State will stand shoulder-to-shoulder with the stories of the organizations and the women who led the national suffrage fight, and it will finally be recognized, and its legacy appreciated.

This book has earnestly attempted to showcase the incredible ladies of Easton and to describe local women's suffrage activities and *why* they happened *this* way *here*. In the stories of Lucy and Chloe and their fellow club members, the churnings of transformation in the roles of women in the modern era are represented. Emerging opportunities for women in politics, education, business, and in the home in turn-of-the-20th century America are mirrored in the lives and work of the Easton ladies. Their commitment to democratic principles and citizenship rights for women put their unique style of *womanly influence* on display. With intellect, femininity, and friendship, they ran their farms, homes, and churches – and fought for equal rights as well. They epitomized the definition of the modern New Woman – unwilling to be left behind in political, economic, educational, and legal affairs while the male population surged forward – and eager to embrace their womanliness in order to influence societal progress.

The story of the Easton Political Equality Club is one of generational appeal and leaves a lasting legacy for the continuing struggles for equality and women's rights today.  Beyond teaching something new about the history of the women's suffrage movement in rural upstate New York, this book shows democracy in action and typifies the magic of *small is beautiful*.   Stories, previously untold, of these suffragists teach us that *there is something extraordinary in the lives of ordinary people*.   And, the orientation of Lucy, Chloe, and the Easton ladies to use the strength of their womanliness – *without compromise* – for their cause is a lesson in the intrinsic benefit of celebrating gender differences in pursuit of the common good.

# NOTES TO CHAPTERS

**Chapter I - Notes:**

*1.    History of Washington County:    Some Chapters in the
History of the Town of Easton* (Washington County Historical
Society, 1959). [Some chapters of this book were written by
members of the Easton Book Club, and also by former members of
the Easton Political Equality Club. In the collection of the Easton
Library, Easton, NY.]

2.    Ibid. [Chloe Sisson's original handwritten history -- and its
transcribed, typed version – of the Political Equality Club is in the
Easton Library, Easton, NY.]

3.    Chloe Sisson's history of the Easton PEC, c. 1921; from the
files of the Easton Library.

4.    Ibid.

5.    Washington County Historical Society, 131.


**Chapter II – Notes:**

1.    Susan E. Barber, "One Hundred Years Toward Suffrage:
An Overview," (2002)
http://memory.loc.gov/anmen/naw/nawsatime.html.

2.    Teri Podnorszki Ulrich, "Suffrage and Feminist Reform In
and Around Warren County," *Pasttimes* (Fall 2004, Vol. VII, No. 4).
[This author is the same author as this book, writing under a previous
name.]

3.    Barber, 1.

4.    Ibid., 1.

5.      Ibid., 1.

6.      Mary Wollstonecraft, *A Vindication of the Rights of Woman* (NY: Modern Library, reprinted 2001).

7.      Ulrich, 3.

8.      Ibid., 3.

9.      Ibid., 3.

10.     Ibid., 3.

11.     Ibid., 3.

12.     Ibid., 3.

13.     Ibid., 3.

14.     Ibid., 4.

15.     Ibid., 4.

16.     Ibid., 4.

17.     Ibid., 4.

18.     Howard Mason, *Backward Glances, Vol. II* (Glens Falls, NY: Webster Mimeoprint Service, 1964), 117.

19.     Ulrich, 4.

20.     Ibid., 4.

21.     Ibid., 4.

22.     Ibid., 4.

23.     Ibid., 4.

24.     Ibid., 4.

25.     Ibid., 4.

26.     Ibid., 5.

27.     Ibid., 5.

28.     Ibid., 5.

29.     Ibid., 5.

30.     Ibid., 5.

31.     Ibid., 5.

32.     Ibid, 5.

33.     Ibid., 5.

34.     Ibid., 5.

35.     *Iron-Jawed Angels*, Copyright© 2004 HBO® , HBO is a registered trademark of Home Box Office, Inc.®

**Chapter III – Notes:**

1.      Kay Stearman, Women's Rights: Changing Attitudes 1900-2000 (Austin, TX: Raintree Stech-Vaughn, 2000), 7.

2.      Ibid., 7.

3.      Simone de Beauvoir, *The Second Sex* (translated by H.M. Parshley, NY: Random House, 1974; reprinted NY: Alfred Knopf, Inc., 1952; original printing 1908), xviii.

4.      Ibid., 376.

5.      Ibid., 456.

6.      Lois W. Banner, *Women in Modern America: A Brief History* (Orlando, FL: Harcourt, Brace, Jovanovich, 1984), 58 – 59.

7.      Washington County Historical Society, 121-122.

8.      Ibid., 114-115.

9.      Ibid., 115.

10.     Ibid., 115.

11.     Ibid., 116.

12.     Ibid., 135.

13.     Easton Political Equality Club Minutes Book, Nov. 20, 1907.

**Chapter IV – Notes:**

1.      *The People's Journal*, Dec. 17, 1891.    [Published in Greenwich, NY.]

2.      "Honor the Ladies," program brochure, by Easton Library, Easton, NY, Oct. 2, 2004.

3.      From Lucy P. Allen's personal composition book, 1909.

4.      *The Washington County Post*, Jan. 27, 1871. [Published in Cambridge, NY.]

5.      Ibid., Jan. 8, 1875.

6.      *The People's Journal*, Oct. 2, 1882.

7.      Ibid., Oct. 19, 1882.

8.      Ibid., Oct. 8, 1891.

9.      Ibid., Oct. 29, 1891.

10.     Ibid.

11.     Ibid., Oct. 22, 1891.

12.     Ibid., Oct. 6, 1892.

13.     Ibid., Mar. 23, 1893.

14.     Ibid., May 11, 1898.

15.     Ibid., Nov. 10, 1892.

16.     Ibid., Feb. 26, 1902.

17.     Easton PEC Minutes Book, 1906 – 1910, Easton Library, Easton, NY.

18.     Ibid.

19.     Ibid., Jun. 27, 1906.

20.     Ibid., Jul. 18, 1906.

21.     Ibid., Aug. 15, 1906.

22.     Ibid., Sept. 19, 1906.

23.     Ibid., Oct. 24, 1906.

24.     Ibid., Nov. 21, 1906.

25.     Ibid., Dec. 18, 1906.

26.     Ibid., Jan. 26, 1907.

27.     Ibid., Feb. 20, 1907.

28.     Ibid., Mar. 21, 1907.

29.     Ibid., May 14, 1907.

30.     Ibid., Jun. 15, 1907.

31.     Ibid., Jul. 18, 1907.

32.     Ibid., Sept. 18, 1907.

33.     Ibid., Nov. 20, 1907.

34.     Ibid., Jan. 18, 1908.

35.     Ibid., Aug. 18, 1908.

36.     Ibid., Sept. 16, 1908.

37.      Ibid., Oct. 21, 1908.

38.      Ibid.

39.      Ibid. Nov. 18, and Dec. 15, 1908.

40.      Ibid., Mar. 17, 1909.

41.      Ibid., May 19, 1909.

42.      Ibid., Jun. 23, 1909.

43.      Ibid., Jun. 23, Jul. 21, and Aug. 18, 1909.

44.      Ibid., Aug. 18, 1909.

45.      Ibid., Oct. 29, 1909.

46.      Ibid., Dec. 15, 1909.

47.      Ibid., Jan. 10,  Apr. 23, and May 10, 1910.

48.      Ibid., May 10, 1910.

49.      Ibid., Apr. 19, 1911.

50.      Ibid., May 17, 1911.

51.      Ibid., Jun. 21, 1911.

52.      Ibid., Aug. 16, 1911.

53.      *The Greenwich Journal*, Jan. 3, 1912.

54.      Ibid., Jan. 24, 1912.

55.      Ibid., Mar. 20, 1918.

56.      Ibid., Aug. 28, 1918.

57.      Ibid., Oct. 2, 1918.

58.      Washington County Historical Society, 131.

59.      Easton PEC Yearbook, 1908-1909. [The yearbooks are in the files of the Easton Library, Easton, NY.]

60.      Easton PEC Yearbook, 1910-1911.

61.      Washington County Historical Society, 131.

**Chapter V – Notes:**

1.      Washington County Historical Society, 76. [Lucy P. Allen wrote this chapter about the Easton Library, of which she was a founder.]

2.      Ibid., 77.

3.      Ibid., 79.

4.      Ibid., 123.

5.      Lucy P. Allen, "Obituary of Chloe A. Sisson," *The Greenwich Journal*, Dec. 1923.

6.      Ibid.

7.      Lucy P. Allen, "III. Of the Suffrage Question," from the papers of Lucy P. Allen in the collection of the Easton Library, Easton, NY. Date not known.

8.      Ibid.

9.      From the papers of Lucy P. Allen in the collection of the Easton Library.

10.      Ibid.

11.      Ibid.

12.      Ibid.

13.      Washington County Historical Society, 129.

**Chapter VI – Notes:**

1.	Teri A. Podnorszki, "The Woman Suffrage Movement in the Glens Falls Area." (Research paper, St. Lawrence University, Canton, NY, 1980), 19. [The author of this paper is the same as this book, writing under a previous name.]

2.	Ibid., 19.

3.	Ibid., 19-20.

4.	Ibid., 20.

5.	Ibid., 20-21.

6.	Ibid., 21.

7.	Ibid., 21-22.

8.	Ibid., 22.

9.	Ibid., 22.

10.	"Tiny Campaigners Are Winning Votes to Send Mama to Albany," *The Tribune*, Aug. 29, 1916.

11.	Ibid.

12.	Podnorszki, 22.

13.	Ibid., 22.

14.	Ibid., 23.

15.	Ibid., 23.

16.	Ibid., 23.

17.	Ibid., 24.

18.	Letter from Elizabeth Wakeman Mitchell to Laura Schafer Porter, Sept. 12, 1917.

19.	R. Paul McCarty, "Laura Schafer Porter – The Women's

Suffrage Movement," in *The Fort Edward Sesquecentennial 1849-1999*, ed. Fort Edward Sesquecentennial Committee (Glens Falls, NY:  Glens Falls Printing, 1999). 17.

20.     Podnorszki, 25.

21.     Ibid., 26.

22.     Ibid., 26.

23.     Letter ftom Gertrude Foster Brown to Laura Schafer Porter, Sept. 17, 1917.

24.     McCarty, 17.

25.     Ibid., 17–20.


**Chapter VII – Notes:**

1.     Fred Daley, "Glens Falls Suffragists Claimed Victory 75 Years Ago," *The Post Star*, Jul. 20, 1995, A1, A7.

2.     Ibid.

3.     From the files of the Warren County Historical Society, Lake George, NY.

4.     Podnorszki, 17-18.

5.     Ibid., 7–8.

6.     *The Warrensburg – Lake George News*, Oct. 26, 1893.

7.     Kathryn E. O'Brien, *The Great and the Gracious on Millionaire's Row* (Sylvan Beach, NY:   North Country Books, 1978), 121-122.

8.     Ibid., 130-132.

9.     William P. Gates, *Millionaire's Row on Lake George, NY* (Queensbury, NY:  W.P. Gates Publishing Co., 2008), 118.

10.     William P. Gates, *Old Bolton on Lake George, NY* (Queensbury, NY: W.P. Gates Publishing Co., 2006), 57.

11.     Notes from a letter to the author from Mary Putnam Jacobi's grandson, Ernst McAneny, Jan. 20, 1980.

12.     Ellen Carol DuBois, "Working Women, Class Relations, and Suffrage Militance: Harriot Stanton Blatch and the New York Woman Suffrage Movement 1894-1909," in *One Woman, One Vote: Rediscovering the Woman Suffrage Movement*, ed. Marjorie Spruill Wheeler (Troutdale, OR: New Sage Press, 1995), 232.

13.     Eleanor Flexner, *Century of Struggle: The Woman's Rights Movement in the United States* (Cambridge: Belknap Press, 1959), 231.

14.     From the files of Lucy P. Allen in the Easton Library, Easton, NY.

15.     Gates (2008), 125.

16.     "Mrs. S. Loines, 99, Suffragist, Dies" *The New York Times*, Apr. 3, 1944.

17.     From the files of the Warren County Historical Society, Lake George, NY.

18.     *The New York Times*, Apr. 3, 1944.

19.     Mabel Keep, ed., *Directory of Women in Civic, Economic, and Educational Affairs in Brooklyn To-Day, 1929-30*. (Bay Terrace, Great Kills, Staten Island, 1930), 9.

20.     Ibid., 9.

21.     Ibid., 13.

22.     Ibid., 13.

23.     Ibid., 15.

24.     From the files of the Warren County Historical Society,

Lake George, NY.

25.      *The New York Times*, Apr. 3, 1944.

26.      Ibid.


**Chapter VIII – Notes:**

1.       Doris Weatherford, *A History of the American Suffragist Movement* (Santa Barbara, CA:  The Moschovitis Group, Inc., 1998), 70.

2.       Abigail Klingbeil, "Women's Rights Movement Has Local Roots," *The Saratogian*, Jul. 12, 1998.

3.       Ibid.

4.       Ibid.

5.       Geneaological information on Susan B. Anthony and Lewis Burtis from Saratoga County Historian's office, Ballston Spa, NY, Nov. 2008.

6.       "Sarah Anthony Burtis Dead," *The New York Times*, Oct. 30, 1900.

7.       From the files of the Saratoga County Historian's Office, Ballston Spa, NY.

8.       From *The Grist Mill* and other files and publications of the Brookside Historical Museum, Ballston Spa, NY

9.       Ibid.

10.      Ibid.

11.      Ibid.

12.      O'Brien, 54-55.

13.      Ibid., 55.

14. Katrina Trask, "Woman Suffrage A Practical Necessity," in *The Woman Citizen*, a publication of *The Woman's Journal*, by the National American Woman Suffrage Association, Oct. 13, 1917, 368-369.

15. Ibid.

16. Ibid.

17. Ibid.

18. George Foster Peabody, "The Big Question Before Us Today, *The Post Star*, Feb. 17, 1917.

19. O'Brien, 45.

**Chapter IX – Notes:**

1. Podnorszki, 26.

2. Ibid., 26-27.

3. *The Saratogian*, Nov. 7, 1917.

4. Podnorszki, 27.

**Chapter X – Notes:**

1. Program for "Honor the Ladies," Easton Library, Easton, NY, Oct. 2, 2004.

2. Ibid.

3. Ibid.

4. Ibid.

# BIBLIOGRAPHY

"A Handsome Victory Won At the District School Meeting Held At Barker's Grove." *The People's Journal* Oct. 12, 1882.

"Albany Woman to Talk on Suffrage." *The Post Star* Feb. 2, 1914.

Allen, Lucy P., "Suffrage Articles," 1909. [In the collection of the Easton Library, Easton, NY.]

*An Introduction to the Historic Resources in Washington County, NY.* Prepared by the Washington County Planning Department for the Washington County Planning Board, sponsored by the Washington County Board of Supervisors, Utica, NY: Dodge-Graphic Press, 1976, 36-41.

"At the PEC Last Saturday Afternoon There Was Much Genuine Interest Manifested in This Movement.' *The People's Journal* Oct. 29, 1891.

"Anti-Suffrage Address Tonight." *The Post Star* May 15, 1915.

"Anti-Suffragists Organize Here." *The Post Star* May 19, 1915.

"Anti-Suffragists Predict Defeat For Suffrage in Eastern States." *The Post Star* May 6, 1915.

"At the Request of the State Women's Rights Association A Meeting Will Be Held At The Seminary To Organize A Political Equality Club." *The People's Journal* Oct. 8, 1891.

Austin, John, interviewed by author via phone, Queensbury, NY, Jan. 1980.

Baker, Jean H. (ed.) Votes For Women: *The Struggle for Suffrage Revisited*. Oxford: Oxford University Press, 2002.

Banner, Lois W.  *Women in Modern America:   A Brief History*. Orlando, FL:  Harcourt, Brace, Jovanovich, Inc. 1984.

Barber, Susan E. (compl.) *One Hundred Years Toward Suffrage:  An Overview.*   http://memory.loc.gov./anmem/naw/nawsatime.html. 2002.

Barker-Benfield, G.J. and Clinton, Catherine. *Portraits of American Women:  Vol. II – From the Civil War to the Present*. NY:  St. Martin's Press, 1991.

"Big Crowd Hears Suffrage Talks." *The Post Star* Oct. 30, 1917.

Birdsall, Stephen T., interviewed by author, Queensbury, NY, Jan. 6, 1980.

Bowden, Mrs. William, interviewed by author via phone, Glens Falls, NY, Jan. 1980.

*Bridging the Years:  Glens Falls, New York 1763-1978*. Glens Falls, NY:  Glens Falls Historical Association, 1978.

Brown, H. (ed.) *History of Warren County*. Glens Falls, NY:  Glens Falls Post Company, 1963.

Bullock, Dora, interviewed by author, Glens Falls, NY, Jan. 9, 1980.

Calarco, Tom.   *The Underground Railroad in the Adirondack Region*. Jefferson, NC:  McFarland and Co., Inc., 2004.

Camhi, Jane Jerome.   *Women Against Women:  American Anti-Suffragism, 1880-1920*. Brooklyn, NY:   Carlson Publishing, Inc., 1994.

Catt, Carrie Chapman, and Shuler, Nettie Rogers.  *Woman Suffrage and Politics*. NY:  Charles Scribner's Sons, 1926.

Clift, Eleanor.   *Founding Sisters and the Nineteenth Amendment*. Hoboken, NJ:  John Wiley and Sons, Inc., 2003.

Collins, Gail.   *America's Women:  Four Hundred Years of Dolls,*

*Drudges, Helpmates, and Heroines.* NY:  William Morrow, 2003.

"Committees for Suffrage Meeting." *The Post Star* Nov. 1, 1917.

*Comprehensive Plan for the Town of Easton.* Easton, NY:   Town Board, 1970.

Conway, Jill K. *The Female Experience in Eighteenth and Nineteenth Century America:  A Guide to the History of American Women. NY:* Garland Publishing, Inc., 1982.

Coolidge, Olivia. *Women's Rights.* NY:  E.P. Dutton and Company, Inc., 1966.

"Correspondence – South Easton." *The People's Journal* Mar. 23, 1893.

Cott, Nancy F. "Across the Great Divide:  Women in Politics Before and After 1920." *One Woman, One Vote:  Rediscovering the Woman Suffrage Movement.* Ed. Marjorie Spruill Wheeler.  Troutdale, OR: New Sage Press, 1995, 353-373.

Cronkhite, James, interviewed by author via phone, Hudson Falls, NY, Jan. 1980.

Crowley, Matthew.  "Suffragettes in the City." *The Post Star* Sept. 14, 1995:  D1, 4.

Cullen-DuPont, Kathryn. *American Women Activist Writings.* NY: Cooper Square Press, 2002.

Daley, Fred.  "Glens Falls Suffragists Claimed Victory 75 Years Ago." *The Post Star* July 20, 1995:  A1, 7.

"Don't Forget to Vote For Woman Suffrage. *The Post Star* Nov. 7, 1917.

Dorr, Rheta Childe. *Susan B. Anthony:  The Woman Who Changed the Mind of a Nation.* NY:  AMS Press, 1970.

"Do Women Want to Vote?" *The Post Star* Jan. 24, 1914.

DuBois, Ellen Carol. *Feminism and Suffrage*. Ithaca, NY: Cornell University Press, 1970.

DuBois, Ellen Carol. "Working Women, Class Relations, and Suffrage Militance: Harriot Stanton Blatch and the New York Woman Suffrage Movement, 1894-1909." *One Woman, One Vote: Rediscovering the Woman Suffrage Movement*. Ed. Marjorie Spruill Wheeler. Troutdale, OR: New Sage Press, 1995, 221-241.

Dworkin, Susan. *She's Nobody's Baby: A History of American Women in the Twentieth Century*. NY: Simon and Schuster, Inc., 1983.

"Easton P.E.C. – Secretary's Reports from April 1906 to Jan. 1908, inclusion 1908-1909-1910." [In the collection of the Easton Library, Easton, NY.]

Eddy, Robert, interviewed by author via phone, Queensbury, NY, Jan. 1980.

Eisenstadt, Peter (ed.) *The Encyclopedia of New York State*. Syracuse, NY: Syracuse University Press, 2005.

Faber, Doris. *Petticoat Politics: How American Women Won the Right to Vote*. NY: Lothrop, Lee, and Shepard Co., Inc., 1967.

Felder, Deborah G. *A Century of Women: The Most Influential Events in Twentieth Century Women's History*. NY: Kensington Press, 1999.

Flexner, Eleanor. *Century of Struggle: The Woman's Suffrage Movement in the United States*. Cambridge: Belknap Press, 1959.

"Frances E. Willard Memorial Service." *The Post Star* Feb. 14, 1914.

Frost, E. and Cullen-DuPont, K. *Women's Suffrage in America: An Eyewitness History*. NY: Facts on File, Inc., 1992.

Gates, William P. *Millionaire's Row on Lake George, NY*. Queensbury, NY: W.P. Gates Publishing Company, 2008.

Gates, William P. *Old Bolton on Lake George, NY.* Queensbury, NY: W.P. Gates Publishing Company, 2006.

Ginzberg, Lori D. *Untidy Origins: A Story of Women's Rights in Antebellum New York.* Chapel Hill, NC: University of North Carolina Press, 2005.

Gleadle, Kathryn. *The Early Feminists: Radical Unitarians and the Emergence of the Women's Rights Movement, 1831-51.* NY: St. Martin's Press, 1995.

"Glens Falls' First Suffrage Meeting." *The Post Star* Jan 7, 1914.

Graham, Sarah Hunter. "The Suffrage Renaissance: A New Image for a New Century, 1896-1910." *One Woman, One Vote: Rediscovering the Woman Suffrage Movement.* Ed. Marjorie Spruill Wheeler. Troutdale, OR: New Sage Press, 1995, 157-178.

"Greenwich Voters Prove Extremely Dry; Women Vote for First Time. *The Greenwich Journal* Oct. 2, 1918: 1.

Griffin, Elisabeth. *In Her Own Right: The Life of Elizabeth Cady Stanton.* NY: Oxford University Press, 1984.

Gurko, Miriam. *The Ladies of Seneca Falls: The Birth of the Women's Rights Movement.* NY: MacMillan Publishing Company, Inc., 1974.

Hall, Mrs. Carter T., letter to author, Jan. 7, 1980.

Hall, Robert F. *Pages from Adirondack History.* Fleischmanns, NY: Purple Mountain Press, 1992, 110-113.

Hallenbeck, Donald, interviewed by author, Glens Falls, NY, Jan. 15, 1980.

Harrington, Rachel, interviewed by author, Glens Falls, NY, Jan. 9, 1980.

Hay, H. (compl.) *A History of Temperance in Saratoga County, New*

*York*. Saratoga Springs, NY:  GM Davison Printing, 1855.

*History of Warren County, New York*. Glens Falls, NY:  Board of Supervisors of Warren County, 1963.

*History of Washington County, New York*.  Philadephia, PA:  J.B. Lippincott and Company, 1872, 290-300.

*History of Washington County, New York – Some Chapters in the History of the Town of Easton, NY*.  The Washington County Historical Society, 1959.

"Honor the Ladies" Exhibit Materials. Oct. 2, 2004. [In the collection of the Easton Library, Easton, NY.]

Hyde, Louis F.  *History of Glens Falls, New York and Its Settlement*. Glens Falls, NY:  The Hyde Collection, 1983.

Jacobi, Dr. Mary Putnam.  *Common Sense Applied to Woman Suffrage*. NY:  G.P. Putnam's Sons, 1894.

Keep, Mabel (ed.)  *Directory of Women in Civic, Economic, and Educational Affairs in Brooklyn To-Day, 1929-30*.  Bay Terrace, Great Kills, Staten Island, 1930.

Klingbeil, Abigail.  "Womens Rights Movement Has Local Roots." *The Saratogian*  Jul. 12, 1998.

Kraditor, Aileen S.  *The Ideas of the Woman Suffrage Movement*. NY: Columbia University Press, 1965.

Krarup, Margaret, interviewed by author via phone, Glens Falls, NY, Jan. 1980.

Leonbruno, Frank.  *Lake George Reflections*. Fleischmanns, NY: Purple Mountain Press, 1998.

"Local Men Speak for Suffrage." *The Post Star* Nov. 1, 1917.

"Local Men Will Talk on Suffrage." *The Post Star* Feb. 27, 1914.

"Local Women to March in Parade." *The Post Star* Oct. 27, 1917.

Lumsden, Linda J.  *Inez:  The Life and Times of Inez Milholland.*
Bloomington, IN:  Indiana University Press, 2004.

Lumsden, Linda J.  *Rampant Women:  Suffragists and the Right of
Assembly.*   Knoxville, TN:  University of Tennessee Press, 1997.

Lutz, Alma.   *Susan B. Anthony:   Rebel, Crusader, and
Humanitarian.*  Washington, D.C.: Zenger Publishing, 1959.

MacEachron, Mrs. Gordon, letter to author, Jan. 17, 1980.

McAneny, Ernst, letter to author, Jan. 20, 1980.

McMillen, Sally G.  *Seneca Falls and the Origins of the Women's
Rights Movement.*  Oxford:  University Press, 2008.

McCarty, R. Paul, interviewed by author, Fort Edward, NY, Jan 24,
1980.

McCarty, R. Paul.  "Laura Schafer Porter – The Women's Suffrage
Movement." *The Fort Edward Sesquecentennial, 1849-1999.*  Glens
Falls,  NY:    Glens  Falls  Printing  and  the  Fort  Edward
Sesquecentennial Committee, 1999, 17-23.

"Makes Plea for Woman's Suffrage. *The Post Star* Jan. 8, 1914.

Mankiller, W., Mink, G., Navarro, M., Smith B. Steinem G. (eds.)
*The Reader's Companion to United States Women's History.*  NY:
Houghton Mifflin Company, 1998.

Marrs, Theresa.  "Springside Buildings to be Surveyed." *The Post
Star*  Mar. 22, 1975.

"Mary Stafford Anthony." *Western NY Suffragists – Biographies and
Images*, http://www.winningthevote.org/Manthony/html.

Mason, Howard C. *Backward Glances, Vol. II.*   Glens Falls, NY:
Webster Mimeoprint Service, 1964.

"Men's League to Canvass County." *The Post Star* Oct. 22, 1917.

"Men of Warren County!" *The Post Star* Nov. 6, 1917.

"Men's Suffrage League Here." *The Post Star* Oct. 17, 1917.

"Minute Book of Easton WCTU, Dec. 4, 1888-Nov. 2, 1893." [In the collection of the Easton Library, Easton NY.]

"Minutes of the Easton Book Club (Sept. 1926- Dec. 1960) – Vol. I." [In the collection of the Easton Library, Easton, NY.]

"Miss Harriet May Mills of Syracuse, Will Speak at the Seminary." *The People's Journal* Apr. 20, 1893.

"Miss Pierson Converts Many." *The Post Star* Jan. 6, 1914.

"Miss Susan B. Anthony Gave A Lecture at the Friends Seminary." *The County Post* Jan. 8, 1875.

Mitchell, Mrs. Willis G. "Woman Suffrage and The Grange." *The Post Star* Feb. 19, 1917.

Morgan, David. *Suffragists and Democrats: The Politics of Woman Suffrage in America.* East Lansing, MI: Michigan University Press, 1972.

"Mr. Voter, Vote 'Yes' on Woman Suffrage Today." *The Post Star* Nov. 7, 1917.

"Mrs. S. Loines, 99, Suffragist, Dies." *The New York Times* Apr. 3, 1944.

Nancy Dalton Rogal, interviewed via phone by Laura Lee Linder, Bolton Landing, NY, Nov. 2, 2008.

"Noted Men Tell Why They Are For Woman Suffrage." *The Post Star* Nov. 1, 1917.

O'Brien, Kathryn E. *The Great and Gracious on Millionaire's Row.* Sylvan Beach, NY: North Country Books, 1978.

"On 16th, Susan B. Anthony Electrified Audience at Friends Seminary." *The County Post* Jan. 27, 1871.

Peabody, Alice Robertson, interviewed by author via phone, Glens Falls, NY, Jun. 21, 2004.

"PEC Meeting – To Give Play – News of Other Societies. *The Greenwich Journal* Jan. 24, 1912.

Podnorszki, Teri A. "The Woman Suffrage Movement in the Glens Falls Area." Canton, NY:  St. Lawrence University, 1980.

"President Wilson and His Cabinet on Woman Suffrage." *The Post Star* Nov. 2, 1917.

"Public Invited to Suffrage Meeting." *The Post Star* Jan. 6, 1914.

"Republican Candidates for County Committee:  Many Women Will Be Named." *The Greenwich Journal* Mar. 17, 1920, 1.

Robertson, Daniel, interviewed by author via phone, Glens Falls, NY, Jun. 16, 2004.

Robertson, Joan, interviewed by author via phone, Lake George, NY, Jan. 1980.

Rogers, Erskine, interviewed by author via phone, Hudson Falls, NY, Jan. 1980.

Rogers, Erskine, letter to author, Jan. 25, 1980.

Rothman, Sheila M. *Woman's Proper Place: A History of Changing Ideals and Practices, 1870 to the Present*. NY:  Basic Books, Inc., 1978.

"Sarah Anthony Burtis Dead." *The New York Times* Oct. 30, 1900.

"Second Suffragette Meeting This Evening." *The Post Star* Feb. 14, 1914.

"See What They Say. *The Post Star* Nov. 5, 1917.

Sherman, Esther, interviewed by author, Hudson Falls, NY, Jan. 15, 1980.

Snyder, Edgar, interviewed by author via phone, Greenwich, NY, Jan. 1980.

"Some of the Influential Women of Easton Have Obtained Upwards of 200 Signatures. *The People's Journal* Jan. 20, 1881.

Stanton, Elizabeth Cady. *Solitude of Self.* Ashfield, MA: Paris Press, 2001.

Stearman, Kaye. *Women's Rights: Changing Attitudes 1900-2000*. Austin, TX: Raintree Stech-Vaughn, 2000.

Stebbins, Homer Adolph. *A Political History of the State of New York 1865-1869*. NY: AMS Press, 1967.

Stevens, Doris. *Jailed for Freedom: American Women Win the Vote*. Troutdale, OR: New Sage Press, 1995.

"Suffrage Calls For New Districts." *The Post Star* Nov. 8, 1917.

"Suffrage Lecture in Girls' Club. *The Post Star* Jan. 31, 1914.

"Suffrage Lectures Draw Large Crowd." *The Post Star* Mar. 2, 1914.

"Suffrage Meeting at Fort Edward." *The Post Star* Nov. 2, 1917.

"Suffrage Meeting at Fort Edward." *The Post Star* Nov. 5, 1917.

"Suffrage Meeting at Greenwich." *The Post Star* Oct. 24, 1917.

"Suffrage Meeting at Hudson Falls." *The Post Star* Oct. 31, 1917.

"Suffrage Meeting Largely Attended." *The Post Star* Jan. 12, 1914.

"Suffrage Meeting Largely Attended." *The Post Star* Jan. 26, 1914.

"Suffrage Meeting Postponed a Week." *The Post Star* Feb. 16, 1914.

"Suffrage Meeting Tomorrow at 2:30." *The Post Star* Oct. 22, 1917.

"Suffrage Section: The Post Star Commemorates the 75th Anniversary of the Woman's Right to Vote." *The Post Star* Feb. 1992.

"Suffragettes to Organize Club." *The Post Star* Mar. 15, 1914.

"Suffragists Are Happy Over Result." *The Post Star* Nov. 7, 1917.

"Suffragists Have Enthusiastic Day." *The Post Star* Nov. 5, 1917.

Suffragists Plan Social Tea Here." *The Post Star* Oct. 16, 1916.

"Suffragists to Meet at Granville." *The Post Star* Oct. 31, 1917.

"Susan B. Anthony in the Greenwich Area." *The Greenwich Journal* Apr. 5, 1979.

"Susan B. Anthony To Be Honored at Women's Meeting." *The Greenwich Journal* Jan. 28, 1948.

Tefft, Grant J. *The Story of Union Village, Vol. II.* Greenwich, NY: The Greenwich Journal, 1943.

"The Annual Meeting of the Easton PEC Will Be Held." *The People's Journal* Oct. 6, 1892.

"The District School Meeting In Town Was More Spirited Than Usual." *The People's Journal* Oct. 9, 1882.

"The Easton PEC Will Meet at the Seminary Saturday Afternoon." *The People's Journal* Oct. 22, 1891.

"The Meeting of the PEC Was Held at Marshall Seminary." *The People's Journal* Feb. 23, 1893.

"The New York State Woman Suffrage Association." *The People's Journal* Nov. 10, 1892.

"The PEC Will Hold Its Next Meeting." *The People's Journal* Dec. 17, 1891.

"The PEC Will Meet With Mrs. Sophia Sisson – Lessons in Civics Will Continue." *The Greenwich Journal* Mar. 20, 1918.

"There Will Be A Political Mass Meeting at Burton Hall." *The*

*Greenwich Journal* Aug. 28, 1918.

"The WCTU and PEC Met in Joint Session." *The Greenwich Journal* Jan. 3, 1912.

"The WCTU of Easton Gave a Memorial Service to Frances Willard." *The People's Journal* May 11, 1898.

"Tiny Campaigners Are Winning Votes to Send Mama to Albany." *The Tribune* Aug. 29, 1916.

"To Speak Against Suffrage Cause." *The Post Star* May 14, 1915.

Trask, Katrina. *In the Vanguard*. NY: The MacMillan Company, 1913.

Trask, Katrina. "Woman Suffrage A Practical Necessity." *The Woman Citizen*, a publication of The Woman's Journal, Oct. 13, 1917, 368-369.

"Two Speakers For Woman Suffrage." *The Post Star* Oct. 27, 1917.

Ulrich, Teri Podnorszki. "Suffrage and Feminist Reform In and Around Warren County. *Pasttimes*. Glens Falls, NY: Warren County Historical Society, Fall 2004, 1, 3-5.

Van Dusen, Richard C. *Glimpses of the Past: Historical Museum Notes*. Glens Falls, NY: Ridgecraft Books, 1970.

Waite, Marjorie Peabody. *Yaddo: Yesterday and Today*. Albany, NY: Argus Press, 1933.

Ward, Geoffrey C. *Not For Ourselves Alone: The Story of Elizabeth Cady Stanton and Susan B. Anthony*. NY: Alfred A. Knopf, 1999.

*Warren County History: A History and Guide*. Glens Falls, NY: Board of Supervisors of Warren County, 1942.

Weatherford, Doris. *A History of the American Suffragist Movement*. Santa Barbara, CA: The Moschovitis Group, Inc., 1998.

"Wednesday the PEC of Easton Met With Mrs. Cornelius Kipp With

28 Present." *The People's Journal*  Feb. 28, 1902.

Weigand, Kate.  *Red Feminism:  American Communism and the Making of Women's Liberation*.  Baltimore, MD:  The Johns Hopkins University Press, 2001.

Wheeler, Marjorie Spruill (ed.).  *One Woman, One Vote: Rediscovering the Woman Suffrage Movement*.  Troutdale, OR:  New Sage Press, 1995.

Whitaker, Jane (compl.) "The Woman Who Started Women's Rights: Susan B. Anthony, 1820-1906." [In the collection of the Greenwich Library, Greenwich, NY.]

"Why I Am For Suffrage." *The Post Star* Oct. 29, 1917.

Wolllstonecraft, Mary.  *A Vindication of the Rights of Woman*.  NY: Modern Library, reprinted 2001.

"Woman Suffrage Speaker Coming." *The Post Star*  Jan. 7, 1914.

"Woman Suffrage Will Help Home." *The Post Star* Jan. 28, 1914.

"Women Lead By 60,000 Majority." *The Post Star*  Nov. 7, 1917.

"Women Urge Suffrage Plank." *The Saratogian*  Sept. 25, 1912.

"Women Win Vote in NY by 90,000 Majority." *The Post Star*  Nov. 8, 1917.

"Your Mother, Your Wife, and Your Daughter." *The Post Star*   Nov. 1, 1917.